Words of Life

Words of Life

A Literary Introduction
to the New Testament

Leland Ryken

BAKER BOOK HOUSE
Grand Rapids, Michigan 49516

Unless otherwise indicated, Scripture quotations are from the Revised Standard
Version Bible, copyright 1946, 1952, 1971 by the Division of Christian Education of
the National Council of the Churches of Christ in the USA, and are used by
permission. The King James Version (KJV) is also cited.

Library of Congress Cataloging-in-Publication Data

Ryken, Leland.
    Words of life.

    Includes indexes.
    1. Bible. N.T.—Criticism, interpretation, etc.
I. Title.
BS2361.2.R94   1987   809'.935225   87-30639
ISBN 0-8010-7747-8

For Nancy

Go and stand in the temple
and speak to the people
all the words
of this Life.
[Acts 5:20]

Contents

Preface

This is a book of literary criticism on the New Testament. It includes three types of material: general comments about the literary nature of the New Testament, literary introductions to the major genres of the New Testament, and explications of specimen texts within these genres. My intention is that this combination of general commentary plus specimen explications will enable a reader to apply the tools of literary analysis to any passage in the New Testament.

This work is a companion to my book *Words of Delight: A Literary Introduction to the Bible,* also published by Baker Book House (1987). At several points in this book on the New Testament the reader will benefit from consulting the companion volume. The literary approach that I develop in this book parallels that in my book *How to Read the Bible as Literature* (Grand Rapids: Zondervan, 1984), but this work contains actual explications of texts lacking in the other book.

For readers wishing more literary commentary on the New Testament, as well as bibliographic suggestions beyond what I provide in this book, I strongly recommend a reference book that I edited entitled *The New Testament in Literary Criticism* (New York: Ungar, 1984). It is an anthology of writings from many New Testament scholars and literary critics.

I am grateful for a sabbatical grant from Wheaton College that facilitated my writing of this book.

Wheaton College
December 1986

1

How Literary Is the New Testament?

The New Testament has suffered from a notable neglect by literary critics. Anthologies of the Bible as literature tend to omit or slight it. The Old Testament is normally felt to be much more literary than the New Testament. Yet when I collected excerpts of literary commentary for a reference book on the New Testament, I was left with the strong impression that the New Testament is no less literary than the Old, and that literary approaches are equally indispensable for understanding both Testaments.[1] The purpose of this opening chapter is to explore what it means that the New Testament is a work of literature and how this affects the way we read and interpret it.

Is the New Testament "Literature"?

The literary status of the New Testament has elicited contradictory claims nearly from the beginning. One of the church fathers, Origen, claimed that the New Testament did not measure up to Greek stan-

1. For a treasury of literary commentary on the New Testament, see Leland Ryken, ed., *The New Testament in Literary Criticism*, A Library of Literary Criticism (New York: Ungar, 1984).

dards of literary style, offering as a reason for this that God wanted it to be clear that the power of the gospel did not rest in human eloquence.[2] Augustine disagreed, stating that Paul's "wisdom is his guide, eloquence his attendant."[3]

Modern Viewpoints

Opinions in our century have followed three main paths. The view that the writers were unlettered people without literary intention or ability, and that they were interested only in the religious content of their utterances, has been prominent. Martin Dibelius writes, for example, that the writers of the New Testament were "men without special education" and that "what they wrote down was either completely unliterary . . . or else half-literary and thus unpretentious writing intended for a certain class of people."[4]

Another major viewpoint is that the New Testament is indeed literary but that its forms are so unique that ordinary literary criteria are powerless to deal with what we find there. The most forceful statement on the uniqueness of New Testament forms is by Amos N. Wilder, who believes that "early Christian literary arts were different from those that ancient paganism produced, and that Greek and traditional humanist categories are inadequate as measuring rods."[5]

Still other commentators have simply operated on the premise that the New Testament has much about it that resembles familiar literary forms of the period in which it was written, or of literature generally. Critics in the former category have lavished attention on trying to identify existing literary models that New Testament writers followed. Critics in the latter camp do not care where or when the literary forms that they find in the New Testament originated, as long as they are genuinely present in the New Testament.

The Approach of This Book

My own approach to the New Testament will stress its literary primacy and show that its literary traits are a mingling of convention

2. Origen, *Against Celsus*, in *The New Testament in Literary Criticism*, p. 16.

3. Augustine, *On Christian Doctrine*, in *The New Testament in Literary Criticism*, p. 17.

4. Martin Dibelius, *A Fresh Approach to the New Testament and Early Christian Literature* (New York: Charles Scribner's Sons, 1936), pp. 16–17. Among the fallacies evident in this viewpoint is the assumption that folk literature cannot be truly literary and artistic. The New Testament proves that it can be.

5. Amos N. Wilder, *Early Christian Rhetoric: The Language of the Gospel* (Cambridge: Harvard University Press, 1971), p. 36. Although Wilder's theory of the uniqueness of New Testament forms is wrong, this book is an excellent source of generalizations about the literature of the New Testament.

and innovation, of the familiar and the new. The four dominant genres of the New Testament—Gospel, Acts, Epistle, and Apocalypse—are unique. We do not find these same generic labels in an anthology of English or American literature, for example. I would insist, though, that the thing that makes these New Testament books unique has a great deal more to do with their content and theological claims than with their form.

To say that New Testament forms are unique obscures an important point. Their uniqueness actually stems from modifications that their writers have made on familiar literary forms. The stories of the Gospels and Acts, the conventions of letter writing in the Epistles, and the visions of the Book of Revelation all draw upon recognizable literary techniques. Old Testament models are particularly relevant for all New Testament forms except the Epistles, where contemporary Greek letters are the basic form on which New Testament writers worked their innovations.

What Makes the New Testament Literary?

The New Testament is literary by the same criteria that we apply to any other canon of literature. The New Testament is more than a work of literature, but it is not less. The writing that we find in the New Testament is a mixture of three types of writing that we find in the Old Testament as well.

One of these is what we might call expository or theological writing, exemplified by the following passage:

> Count it all joy, my brethren, when you meet various trials, for you know that the testing of your faith produces steadfastness. And let steadfastness have its full effect, that you may be perfect and complete, lacking in nothing. [James 1:2–4]

The implied purpose of such theological exposition is to convey information as clearly and directly as possible. The structure and logic of the passage are mainly conceptual; the passage is a sequence of ideas. The vocabulary is predominantly abstract.

A second type of writing in the New Testament is historical writing. The following example is typical:

> After this Paul stayed many days longer, and then took leave of the brethren and sailed for Syria, and with him Priscilla and Aquila. At Cenchreae he cut his hair, for he had a vow. And they came to Ephesus, and he left them there; but he himself went into the synagogue and argued with the Jews. [Acts 18:18–19]

It is not hard to infer that the intended purpose of such a passage is to record the facts of events. I call this the documentary impulse. It is pervasive in the narrative parts of the New Testament (the Gospels and the Book of Acts).

But there is a third type of writing as well, one that with good reason we can call literature. It is usually mingled with the two impulses already noted—the didactic impulse to teach theological and moral truth and the historical impulse to state what actually happened. Although this mixture makes the Bible a unique book, this should not be allowed to obscure the ways in which the New Testament is a literary book by ordinary literary standards. Not to recognize this is to impoverish and misunderstand the New Testament. My purpose in the remainder of this chapter is to suggest the ways in which the New Testament is literary in nature.

Experiential Concreteness

To begin, it is common to define literature partly by its content. The subject of literature is human experience. Literature images reality. It incarnates its meaning in the form of images, characters, and events. Its aim is not to state ideas but to recreate experiences. It accomplishes this aim by appealing to our imagination (the image-making and image-perceiving capacity that we all possess). Literature recreates an experience in sufficient detail and concreteness to enable a reader to relive it.

Because the New Testament shows the characteristic biblical tendency toward the brief unit, it is easy to overlook how concrete its writing is and how many appeals to the imagination it contains. Here is an illustration:

> On that day, when evening had come, [Jesus] said to them, "Let us go across to the other side." And leaving the crowd, they took him with them in the boat, just as he was. And other boats were with him. And a great storm of wind arose, and the waves beat into the boat, so that the boat was already filling. But he was in the stern, asleep on the cushion; and they woke him and said to him, "Teacher, do you not care if we perish?" And he awoke and rebuked the wind, and said to the sea, "Peace! Be still!" And the wind ceased, and there was a great calm. [Mark 4:35–39]

The first thing to note about the passage is that it communicates its truth by means of a story. Meaning is here incarnated or embodied in characters doing things in a particular setting. Despite its brevity, this story is filled with appeals to our image-making capacity. It is full of precision. We know when the action occurs, for example: *when evening had come.* The realism is enhanced by the detail that Jesus joined the others *just as he was.* The waves, we are told with equal vividness, *beat into the boat.* Jesus, moreover, was *asleep on the cushion.* The whole scene comes alive in our imaginations as we read.

All of this concreteness makes it easy to find recognizable human experience in the story. One level of truth in the story is truthfulness to human experience, and this is always a touchstone of literature. We recognize the physical reality of the storm, for example. The psychological experience of terror in the face of physical threat is equally apparent. A literary narrative like this is primarily interested in getting us to relive an experience, not to grasp an idea.

This impulse to image the truth and draw upon everyday experience in the process is not limited to the stories of the New Testament but is just as characteristic of many of the expository sections. Jesus' usual style of preaching or teaching, for example, was heavily anecdotal and poetic (imagistic). The idea of being heavenly-minded becomes as tangible as a drawer full of valuables when Jesus says,

> Do not lay up for yourselves treasures on earth, where moth and rust consume and where thieves break in and steal, but lay up for yourselves treasures in heaven, where neither moth nor rust consumes and where thieves do not break in and steal. [Matt. 6:19–20]

What about the Epistles? Aren't they predominantly abstract? They are much more concrete and experiential than we ordinarily think. For one thing, they are occasional letters written on specific occasions and dealing with specific situations that had arisen in the lives of a church or an individual. They are rarely systematic treatises on a theological issue. This at once gives them an experiential feel.

Beyond this, the very language of the Epistles is frequently concrete and imagistic:

> Share in suffering as a good soldier of Christ Jesus. . . . An athlete is not crowned unless he competes according to the rules. It is the hard-working farmer who ought to have the first share of the crops. [2 Tim. 2:3, 5–6]

The concept of Christian living is much more than an abstraction in such a passage. In a manner typical of literary authors, the writer here uses everyday experiences to express his idea.

When measured by the familiar literary criterion of experiential content, the New Testament is a literary book. It continuously appeals to our intelligence through our imagination. It is abstract in some parts, but its more characteristic mode is presentation of human experience.

Literary Genres

The most customary way to define literature is by its genres (types). Through the centuries, people who deal with literary texts have agreed that certain genres should be classified as literary.

The New Testament is made up of three main genres: narrative or story, letter or epistle, and vision or apocalypse. All three of these tend to be literary rather than expository in nature. Within these broad categories, moreover, we find an abundance of familiar literary forms: parable, oration, proverb or saying, lyric, hymn, and satire.

I noted earlier that the four main classifications of books in the New Testament—the Gospels, Acts, the Epistles, and Revelation—do not have exact parallels in the familiar landscape of English and American literature. But each of them has enough affinities with familiar literary forms to allow us to apply many of the usual categories of story and poetry to them. The Book of Revelation, for example, is hardly a typical story, but the standard narrative questions of who does what, and where, and with what results, are the right ones to ask when dealing with the book.

The uniqueness of the New Testament lies not so much in the individual genres but in the mixture of forms that we find. The Gospels, for example, mingle history, story, drama, oratory, proverb, parable, and poetry in a way that is without exact parallel elsewhere in literature. The Sermon on the Mount combines the techniques of oratory, satire, parable, and poetry. The Book of Revelation combines features of the epistle, poetic symbolism, apocalyptic and visionary writing, drama, and lyric.

Artistry

Literature is an art form. One of the criteria by which we classify something as literary is the presence of form, beauty, craftsmanship, and technique. These qualities can characterize a whole work or only a part of it, but wherever they are strongly in evidence, we rightly consider a text to have literary properties.

In its grandest design, such artistry is evident in the overall structure of individual New Testament books. The Gospel of Matthew, for example, alternates blocks of narrative with blocks of teaching material, and the sections of teaching end with a formula to the effect, "When Jesus had finished these sayings. . . ." In the Gospel of Mark, both the chronology and the symbolic use of setting are based on a principle of Christ's acceptance in Galilee and eventual rejection in Jerusalem, with a literal and symbolic journey between the two. The Book of Acts is structured as a successive series of expanding waves of church movement from Jerusalem to Rome. The Epistles are built on a principle of salutation-thanksgiving-body-moral exhortation-conclusion. The Book of Revelation is structured as an intricate series of sevenfold units.

From such grand architectonics we can move to artistry on a small scale. Here we can note the adherence of individual stories, as well as the parables of Jesus, to such narrative principles as unity, completeness, repetition, and contrast. The discourses of Jesus and many passages in the Epistles are arranged so rhythmically and rhetorically as to qualify as Hebrew poetry:

> What is sown is perishable,
>   what is raised is imperishable.
> It is sown in dishonor,
>   it is raised in glory.
> It is sown in weakness,
>   it is raised in power.
> It is sown a physical body,
>   it is raised a spiritual body. [1 Cor. 15:42–44]

Patterned writing like this is common in the New Testament. Word patterns and image patterns are customary.

What functions are served by such artistry in the New Testament? It heightens the impact of utterance, giving it a force that it would otherwise lack. But it is also delightful in itself. It adds to the enjoyment of our reading of the New Testament. Such writing calls attention to itself by its skill and eloquence. A literary approach differentiates itself from other approaches by placing a high value on the artistic quality of the writing. It is not hesitant to speak of the authors' craftsmanship and to delight in it.

Literary critics assume self-conscious artistry and composition on the part of New Testament writers. In this they differ from many biblical scholars, who either doubt that the writers had literary abilities or are indifferent to the evidence that they did. A common bias of New Testament scholarship is that "we must assume unliterary beginnings of a religious unpretentious 'literature'. . . . We should look in vain for analogies in literature proper."[6]

But why would we make such an assumption? The New Testament

6. Martin Dibelius, *From Tradition to Gospel* (New York: Charles Scribner's Sons, 1935), p. 39.

was written by people steeped in the Old Testament, which is one of the most literary books in the world. These same writers lived in a cultural setting that included the influence of Greek civilization. Paul quotes from Greek writers in the New Testament.[7] Since he did not have *Bartlett's Familiar Quotations* to aid him, we can conclude that he had a firsthand acquaintance with Greek literature and knew some of it by heart. Everywhere we turn in the New Testament we find similarities to Greek literature as well as to Old Testament literature, despite the innovations that we find worked on these conventional forms. The New Testament epistles bear resemblances to Hellenistic letters, the Epistle of James to the Greek form known as the diatribe, the Book of Revelation to Greek dramatic conventions. The prologue to the Gospel of John is partly a parody of the Greek *Hymn to Zeus*. The speeches of Paul in Acts are similar to classical orations and defense speeches.[8]

Literary Language

Literature in general, and poetry in particular, use special resources of language in a way that we can recognize as literary. The most obvious category is figurative language. We can consider a passage to be literary whenever the writer makes use of metaphor, simile, symbol, hyperbole, apostrophe, personification, allusion, paradox, pun, or irony. New Testament writing is continuously figurative in these ways.

The most famous example is the discourses of Jesus:

> Beware of false prophets, who come to you in sheep's clothing but inwardly are ravenous wolves. You will know them by their fruits. Are grapes gathered from thorns, or figs from thistles? So, every sound tree bears good fruit, but the bad tree bears evil fruit. [Matt. 7:15–17]

But such a reliance on figurative language, especially metaphor and symbol, is also common in the Epistles:

> For the sun rises with its scorching heat and withers the grass; its flower falls, and its beauty perishes. So will the rich man fade away in the midst of his pursuits. [James 1:11]

7. See, for example, 1 Corinthians 15:33, which is quoted from the play *Thais* by the Greek dramatist Menander; the speech to the Areopagus in Acts 17, where Paul alludes to Homer, Cleanthes, Aratus, and Epimenides; and Titus 1:12, where he quotes with approval from the Cretan poet Epimenides.
8. These and similar points are made by the authors in *The New Testament in Literary Criticism*.

And as for the Book of Revelation, its essential mode is symbolism:

> " 'He who conquers, I will make him a pillar in the temple of my God;
> ... and I will write on him the name of my God, and the name of the
> city of my God....' " [3:12]

The language of the New Testament is generally much more concrete in its original than it is in modern English translations. A literary approach is sensitive to these energies of language. In 2 Peter 1:5, for example, we are commanded to "supplement" our faith with various virtues. This looks abstract until we learn that the term had a special meaning in its original usage.[9] Wealthy patrons of Greek plays had a practice of paying the expenses for equipping and training actors. To "supplement" faith with virtues is far from an abstraction. It means generous and costly cooperation and is as palpable as lavishly equipping a group of actors.

The special resources of language employed by New Testament writers also include rhetorical patterns and devices. I have noted that many prose passages are so patterned and display such parallelism that they should be printed in the form of Hebrew poetry. In addition to such symmetry of clauses, we find rhetorical questions, question-and-answer constructions, imaginary dialogues, and patterns of repetition. Most notable of all is the aphoristic tendency of the New Testament—its richness in proverbs or "sayings," often figurative in expression, that compress a great deal more meaning into them than ordinary discourse does.[10]

The important principle at work here is that such language patterns allow writers to communicate more than ordinary language conveys. Such writing stands out. It has arresting strangeness. It overcomes the cliché effect of ordinary language. Skill with language is a literary feature that is prominent in the New Testament.

A corollary of this special use of language is that style can become an avenue for a literary approach to the New Testament. The letter or epistle, for example, may not be an inherently literary form, but the stylistic excellence of the New Testament epistles invites a literary approach (among other approaches). Many of the individual episodes

9. My information comes from Michael Green, *The Second Epistle General of Peter and the General Epistle of Jude*, Tyndale New Testament Commentaries series (Grand Rapids: Eerdmans, 1968), pp. 66–67.

10. For more on the ways in which the sayings of Jesus use literary resources to convey more than ordinary discourse does, I especially recommend Robert C. Tannehill, *The Sword of His Mouth: Forceful and Imaginative Language in Synoptic Sayings* (Philadelphia: Fortress, 1975).

in the Gospels are too brief and unembellished to seem like literary narratives, but their realistic style and the presence of Jesus' memorable sayings in them makes them literary.

Master Images or Archetypes

The literary imagination organizes reality around recurrent master images known as archetypes. An archetype is an image, character type, or plot motif that recurs throughout literature (as well as throughout life). Archetypes are the building blocks of literature and the ingredients of our own lives.

Here, too, the New Testament adheres to literary principles. Images such as light and darkness, bread and water, blood and cross pervade the pages of the New Testament. Archetypal character types are equally prominent. For example, the suffering servant, the outcast, the refuser of festivities (usually in the form of the Jews and the Pharisees), master and servant, and the pilgrim are recurrent figures in the New Testament. Among plot motifs, images of journey, quest, initiation, the lost and found, death and resurrection are prominent. Jesus' parables are especially rich in archetypes.

The importance of these archetypes is multiple. They are a leading means by which the New Testament emerges in our imagination and thinking as a unified book. They also help to familiarize modern readers with a book that in many ways seems remote from their own lives. They enhance our understanding of the universal human implications of what is recounted in the New Testament. Finally, these master images embody much of the religious meaning that the New Testament writers wished to express.

A Literary Approach to the New Testament

The New Testament is inherently literary at the levels of both form and content. At the level of content, its authors show more interest in recreating experiences and conveying truth by means of particular images than in developing abstract ideas. At the level of form, it shows its literary allegiance by the prevalence of literary genres, a high degree of artistry, special resources of language, and the presence of unifying master images.

These literary features do not guarantee a literary approach to the New Testament. As I noted earlier, the New Testament is a hybrid form that mingles history, theological exposition, and literature. It invites a multiplicity of approaches. What, then, characterizes a literary approach to the New Testament?

Literary commentary is alive to the images and experiential concreteness of the New Testament. It resists the impulse to reduce literary texts to abstract propositions or to move beyond the text to the history behind it. This means a willingness to accept the text on its own terms and to concentrate on reliving the experiences that are presented. A literary approach assumes that much of the meaning of the New Testament is communicated by means of characters, events, and images.

This literary stance implies a whole methodology. It assumes that a text invites us to enter a whole world of the imagination and to live in that world before we move beyond it. A basic premise of literary interpretation is that, in the words of novelist Flannery O'Connor, "the whole story is the meaning, because it is an experience, not an abstraction."[11] To read in a literary way is to use our imaginations to enter a whole world having its own settings, characters, events, customs, ideas, and symbols. These are the means by which a literary text communicates its meanings. They appeal to what modern psychology calls the right side of the brain—our capacity to take in the truth imagistically, experientially, intuitively, and wholistically.

Believing that the subject of literature is human experience, a literary approach is particularly attuned to the universal meanings in a text. It operates on the premise that whereas history tells us what happened, literature tells us what happens. A literary approach assumes that characters in a story have a burden of meaning larger than themselves. They are representatives of the human condition generally. A main purpose of literary criticism of the New Testament is therefore to build bridges between the New Testament world and our own experiences.

Literary critics also believe that a text must be approached in an awareness of its genre. An awareness of genre, in fact, programs how we assimilate and organize a text. The right interpretation of a text, writes a literary critic, is the one "that conforms to the intentionality of the book itself and to the conventions it assumes and requires."[12] The key idea here is the emphasis on intentionality of the book, implying a generic approach, in contrast to the usual claims of biblical scholars to know the intention of the author.

A literary approach is equally interested in artistic form, both as something that enhances the impact and meaning of an utterance and as something that is beautiful and delightful in itself. To the literary

11. Flannery O'Connor, *Mystery and Manners,* ed. Sally and Robert Fitzgerald (New York: Farrar, Straus and Giroux, 1957), p. 73.
12. Northrop Frye, *The Great Code: The Bible and Literature* (New York: Harcourt Brace Jovanovich, 1981), p. 80.

critic, it is not a matter of indifference that the parables and discourses of Jesus are among the most beautiful literary passages in the world. The eloquence of many passages in the Epistles, the storytelling ability of the writer of Acts, and the imagistic splendors of the Book of Revelation are things in which the literary critic is interested.

An attention to the nuances of language is also part of a literary approach to the New Testament. Literary critics believe that much of the language of the New Testament is essentially poetic, consisting of images, metaphors, and other figurative expressions that require ordinary tools of poetic analysis for the unfolding of their meanings. In addition to individual images and metaphors are the overriding master images that both unify the New Testament and convey important aspects of its religious meaning.

Much of what I have said about a literary approach to the New Testament can be summarized under the formula *meaning through form*. This simply asserts that we cannot derive the meaning of the New Testament without first examining its form. "Form" should be construed broadly in this context. It includes anything that involves how a writer has expressed his content, as distinct from what he has said. Without form (beginning, of course, with language itself), no meaning is conveyed.

While this is true for all forms of writing, it is especially crucial for literature. Literary discourse has its own forms or "language," and these tend to be more complex, subtle, and indirect than ordinary discourse. The storyteller, for example, speaks with characters, action, and setting. This means that before we can understand what storytellers are saying about reality we must first interact with the form, that is, the story. In a similar way, poetry conveys its meanings through figurative language. It is therefore impossible to talk about what a poetic statement means without first encountering the form (metaphor or simile, for example).

The literary critic's preoccupation with the "how" of New Testament writing is therefore not frivolous. It is evidence of an aesthetic delight in artistic form, but it is more than that. It is also evidence of a desire to understand what is said in the New Testament, in keeping with its tendency to incarnate meaning in literary forms that require careful scrutiny.

Distinctive Literary Features of the New Testament

I hope that this book will show readers that the New Testament is in many ways like the literature with which they are familiar. A story is a story, after all, wherever we encounter it. One reason why many modern readers lack the antennae to respond to the New Testament is that it has traditionally been isolated from the familiar landscape of their reading experience. Along with these familiar features, however, it is also beneficial to note at the outset some distinctive features that characterize the New Testament as a literary book.

For example, the New Testament is from start to finish a religious book. It represents literature in the service of a didactic purpose. There is a strong rhetorical or persuasive purpose behind the writing. The New Testament is a literature of encounter and confrontation, presupposing response as a condition of reading it. Erich Auerbach long ago noted the prevalence (without parallel in other ancient literature) of face-to-face dialogues in the New Testament.[13]

The New Testament shares this religious quality with the Old Testament, but what is distinctive to the New Testament is its specifically Christocentric focus. The most obviously distinctive feature of the Gospels, for example, is their consistent concentration on the person and work of Christ. The Book of Revelation, which in its opening statement of theme announces that it is the revelation or unveiling of Jesus Christ, is likewise constructed around Jesus as protagonist. The Book of Acts and the Epistles focus on the world-changing impact of the redemptive life of Christ in the early church.

Another distinguishing literary feature of the New Testament is its simplicity and realism. The simplicity is a simplicity of majesty, but both the language and the style are relatively unembellished (with some passages in the Epistles serving as exceptions). Combined with this simplicity is realism. The writers of the New Testament deliberately include everyday details in their accounts. The New Testament keeps us firmly rooted in our familiar world, not only in the narratives but in the discourses of Jesus and the Epistles as well. As we read the New Testament we live in a world of farming and nature and buying and selling and journeying. Auerbach describes it as "a world which is . . . entirely real, average, identifiable as to place, time, and circumstances" (p. 43).

But by some mysterious transformation, these realistic and precise images point beyond themselves to spiritual realities. In the New Testament, words become more than words. There is an incipient symbolism at work. Sowing seed and baking bread and putting on armor become more than physical activities. The concrete sensory world con-

---

13. Erich Auerbach, *Mimesis: The Representation of Reality in Western Literature,* trans. Willard R. Trask (Princeton: Princeton University Press, 1953), p. 46. Wilder, *Early Christian Rhetoric,* pp. 40–54, also has good comments on the confrontational quality of the New Testament.

tinuously opens into a spiritual world, usually conceived as the kingdom of God. The New Testament is preeminently a literature of "second meanings" in which there is almost always more than meets the eye.

The New Testament is also strongly oral. Most of what we read almost certainly existed first in oral form. Jesus himself wrote nothing of what we find in the New Testament. Oral forms such as addresses, sayings, and dialogues dominate the narrative parts of the New Testament (the Gospels and Acts), whose individual units probably circulated orally before being collected in written documents. The Epistles, though they were written, are strongly oral in their rhetoric and were for the most part intended for public reading. The same is true of the Book of Revelation. Wilder summarizes the situation aptly: "Oral speech is where it all began. . . . Even when [the writers] did come to write we can overhear the living voices, speaking and praising. This kind of writing is very close to speech" (p. 40).

The oral roots of New Testament literature help to explain another literary feature—the fact that the New Testament is popular or folk literature. It speaks to the common person. In the words of a biblical scholar, the New Testament is "the Book of the People."[14] Its language is for the most part the language of everyday speech. Its writers show a preference for the brief unit that is easily grasped. The Gospels and the Book of Acts, for example, are not single sustained stories but collections of stories. The informal nature of the Epistles—indeed, even the choice of the letter as a form—shows that they arose from real-life situations and were addressed to ordinary people. And the Book of Revelation, replete with animal characters and battles and dragons, sprang "not from the professional scribes or the official class," being rather "for the most part folk-literature."[15] The folk-literature quality of the New Testament reaches its high point with the parables of Jesus, which are the very touchstone of the popular imagination as it has existed through the centuries.

A final trait that we might notice is that the New Testament is not a self-contained book. It presupposes the Old Testament as a condition of understanding it. Its writers repeatedly treat the events about which they write as the fulfillment of Old Testament prophecies. The New Testament is filled with echoes of the Old Testament. Northrop Frye has expressed the situation accurately when he notes that New Testament references to the Old

---

14. Adolf Deissmann, *Light from the Ancient East*, trans. Lionel R. M. Strachan (New York: Harper and Brothers, 1927), p. 145.

15. Isbon T. Beckwith, *The Apocalypse of John: Studies in Introduction with a Critical and Exegetical Commentary* (New York: Macmillan, 1919), p. 171.

extend over every book—not impossibly every passage—in the New Testament; and some New Testament books . . . are a dense mass of such allusions, often with direct or oblique quotations. . . . The New Testament . . . claims to be, among other things, the key to the Old Testament, the explanation of what the Old Testament really means (p. 79).

The New Testament, then, emerges as a combination of the familiar and the unfamiliar. At many points it invites comparison with familiar literature. Elsewhere, especially at the level of content, it is a unique book.

2

The Gospels

The four New Testament Gospels contain the same three ingredients that are intermingled throughout the Bible: the historical impulse to record the facts, the theological and didactic impulse to teach religious truth, and the literary impulse to recreate experiences in our imaginations. In this important sense they are thoroughly similar to other narrative parts of the Bible. The Gospels' distinctiveness within the Bible has a great deal more to do with content (especially the characterization of Jesus and the nature of his message) than with literary form.

The Gospel as a Literary Form

It is generally claimed that the Gospels are a unique form and that there is no model to which they can be adequately compared. The claims for the uniqueness of the Gospels are not misguided, but they have been overstated. The Gospels are encyclopedic forms, and it is the precise combination of literary elements that converge in them that is without precise parallel outside of the Bible.

The combination of individual forms that make up the Gospels is truly striking. The list of genres represented in the Gospels keeps expanding as we analyze these books. Historical narrative, parable, drama or dialogue, sermon or oration, and saying or proverb are especially prominent. In addition, the Gospels remind us at various points of biography, diary or journal, tragedy, comedy, satire, and poetry. There is nearly equal emphasis on what happened (narrative) and what was said (discourse). Where else in our literary experience, or even within the Bible, do we find exactly this combination?

How Literary Are the Gospels?

A good starting point for a literary approach to the Gospels is to explore what makes them literary. If we simply apply the criteria for determining literariness that I discussed in the opening chapter of this book, we will see at once that the Gospels are very literary in nature.

To begin, they are filled with vivid details that appeal to our imaginations and allow us to recreate experiences as we read. The writers consistently go beyond the documentary impulse to record the bare historical facts. They also want us to experience the events. Here is the type of passage that epitomizes the Gospels:

> On another sabbath, when he entered the synagogue and taught, a man was there whose right hand was withered. And the scribes and the Pharisees watched him, to see whether he would heal on the sabbath, so that they might find an accusation against him. But he knew their thoughts, and he said to the man who had the withered hand, "Come and stand here." And he rose and stood there. And Jesus said to them, "I ask you, is it lawful on the sabbath to do good or to do harm, to save life or to destroy it?" And he looked around on them all, and said to him, "Stretch out your hand." And he did so, and his hand was restored. [Luke 6:6–10]

We see here the usual biblical preference for the brief unit rather than the embellished story, but it is amazing how many appeals there are to our imagination. We visualize the setting and events. There is a wealth of specific detail regarding human gestures and what the characters actually said. Like many another passage from the Gospels, this episode is ready for filming. It comes alive in our imaginations and thereby obeys the most primary of all literary impulses.

Literature does not present its material objectively but always offers an interpretation of the human experiences that it presents. Here, too, the Gospels show a literary inclination. Each of the four Gospels has its distinctive world, its own preoccupations, its own assumed audience, its own picture of Jesus and his teaching. The story of Jesus is told from four different points of view, as scholars have repeatedly shown.

A third criterion of literature is that it presents its content in a highly artistic form. In stories, such artistry consists of pattern, unity, balance, symmetry, contrast, foil, repetition, foreshadowing, and echo. In the Gospels, this artistry is plentiful. It ranges from such small things as the arrangement of individual units into a meaningful pattern, to such large matters as the overall structure of a Gospel.

As an example of the former, the genealogy that opens the Gospel of Matthew (1:1–16) falls into three segments of fourteen names each, a pattern that the writer himself points out (v. 17). For artistry on a grand scale, we can observe the structure of Matthew as a whole. It is a symphonic design in which units of narrative and units of teaching alternate. The five blocks of teaching material, moreover, end with a refrain along the lines of "when Jesus had finished these sayings" (see 7:28; 11:1; 13:53; 19:1; 26:1). The instances of such careful patterning in the Gospels are truly impressive.[1]

To sum up, the Gospels are thoroughly literary in nature. They have been such a frequent source for sermons that we tend to think of them as collections of unrelated fragments. The best antidote to this misconception is to read whole Gospels at a single sitting, conscious of the definition of literature that I have given.

Narrative as the Primary Form

It came as quite a surprise to me to learn that biblical scholarship in our century has generally regarded the discourse or saying as the primary form of the Gospels. This no doubt stemmed from the preoccupation of scholars with the original form that the Gospels took. That form was oral and consisted of the preaching of the apostles about Jesus. From these oral fragments the Gospels as we now find them evolved.

But if we simply look at the four Gospels as we now have them, it is obvious that above all they tell a story. Narrative is the organizing framework within which the sayings and discourses are arranged. The reason the Gospels remain collections of incoherent fragments in most people's minds is that not enough attention has been given to their story qualities.

As stories, the Gospels are episodic rather than unified around a single progressive action in which one event leads to the next. Once we become accustomed to this arrangement, its virtues as a way of telling the story of Jesus become obvious. The apparent randomness effectively portrays Jesus in his manifold roles. The writers show us

1. For a sampling, see the entries on the individual Gospels in Leland Ryken, ed., *The New Testament in Literary Criticism*, A Library of Literary Criticism (New York: Ungar, 1984).

the many sides of Jesus, which would be hard to do by portraying a single action.

This same randomness also conveys a general sense of the life Jesus lived. The variety of scenes, events, and characters captures the nature of the world in which Jesus lived and acted. Stop to consider Jesus' life during the years of his public ministry: he traveled, preached, led a group of disciples, performed miracles, engaged in dialogue with people, defended his actions and beliefs in open debate, and was finally put on trial and crucified. Given the many-sided nature of his life, the mixture and arrangement of ingredients that we find in the Gospels capture the reality of Jesus' life better than more traditional conceptions of plot.

The sheer variety, instead of impairing the unity of the Gospels, actually supports it. All that appears in the Gospels bears the stamp of Jesus' life and world. An inner consistency emerges in our imaginations. We come to expect that something different will happen every few minutes as we read.

Unity in the Gospels

The most important unifying factor in the Gospels is unity of hero. Everything in the Gospels focuses on the person, acts, and sayings of Jesus, and this is one of the chief identifying traits of the genre.

Although the Gospels are not strictly chronological, they are loosely so. The general pattern is a movement from Jesus' birth (which is recorded only in Matthew and Luke), through his three-year earthly ministry, to his death, followed by his resurrection. All four Gospels are structured in such a way as to make the passion of Jesus (the events surrounding his crucifixion) the climax toward which the story moves.

Within this general chronological framework, the individual Gospel writers arranged their material to fit their specific thematic and narrative purposes. Matthew and Mark, for example, both record a day of teaching in parables, but Mark places it near the beginning of his story (chap. 4) and Matthew halfway through his (chap. 13). Some of the events in Jesus' life appear in different places in the different Gospels. John, for example, placed Jesus' cleansing of the temple near the beginning of his story (chap. 2), whereas the three synoptic Gospels have it near the end of the book during the Passion Week.

The arrangement of material in the Gospels will seem more unified if we pause to consider that it reflects how the memory recalls events. Memory was important in the composition of the Gospels, which no doubt represent the final molding of material that first circulated orally in the form of individual units. How does the memory work? It recalls broad outlines, it remembers single incidents, and it strings together certain sequences of events. This is exactly what we find in the Gospels. The Gospels are structured on the principle of memory.

The Gospels are further unified by recurrent situations or type scenes. Jesus is always the central figure in the scene. Next to him in importance is the group of disciples. Almost as prominent are the Pharisees, a nearly constant force of hostility. Another rather constant group is the crowd of ordinary people, sometimes a nameless mass, at other times represented by a particular named person.

The crowds are normally caught between the claims of Jesus and the authority of the religious establishment. As a result of this middle position, the crowds are typically poised at a moment of choice. Jesus is usually shown trying to persuade them, either by word or miracle or disparagement of his enemies. Given this implied struggle for the minds of the onlookers, we can see why Jesus and the Pharisees so often initiated conflict with each other.

If characters help to unify the Gospels, so does geography. In each Gospel we enter a narrative world replete with place names. We are constantly in the world of Palestine as we travel with Jesus from one locale to another. Sometimes the geography is used for structural purposes. The Gospel of Mark, for example, is structured on a grand contrast between Galilee, place of acceptance, and Jerusalem, which symbolizes rejection of Jesus.

Individual episodes within the Gospels are unified by the same principles of narrative unity that we find in any story. The right questions to ask are the usual ones of setting, characterization, and plot, namely, Where? Who? What happens? The commonest structural principle in the individual episodes of the Gospels is that of conflict moving toward resolution. Even if there is not a conflict, we should be alert for a progression toward a final resolution or moment of epiphany, as in the story of Jesus' encounter with the woman at the well (John 4:1–30).

Because the Gospels contain so much dialogue and encounter, it is also a helpful procedure for many of the episodes to lay out the action into separate dramatic scenes, as though it were a play, focusing on each segment and also noting the sequence or positioning of scenes as we move through the episode. As a variation on this procedure, we might profitably approach some of the episodes as though the event were being photographed by a television crew. We will find distant or overview shots, close-ups, shifts from one speaker to another, shots of the crowd, and so forth.

Still more unity emerges if we pay attention to the narrative world around which each Gospel is constructed. It is a literary principle that works of literature create their own consistent world of interrelated details. The individual Gospels have their own characteristic ideas, images, settings, and emphases. In Matthew's Gospel, for example, we move in a Jewish world where Old Testament prophecies and religious customs are consistently present, where Jesus is repeatedly portrayed in terms of royalty, and where the teaching of Jesus is organized into blocks interspersed between sections of narrative. With Luke's Gospel we enter a different narrative world—a cosmopolitan world in which people on the social and religious fringes (women, the poor, outsiders, people in shady occupations) are the ones who receive God's grace. Knowing that individual Gospel writers build their own world in this way can go a long way toward unifying our experiences of the Gospels.

The Portrait of Jesus

The Gospels exist to explain the life and message of Jesus. It is possible, however, to misinterpret how the writers went about their task. There are three theories on the matter. We might compare them to three types of visual art—a photograph, a painted portrait, and an abstract painting.[2] A photograph records everything about a subject and is virtually objective. Its limitation is that it cannot be very interpretive of the subject, nor can it highlight a given aspect of the subject. A painted portrait is selective in details, highlighting certain aspects of a subject while omitting others. An abstract painting conveys only a vague impression of its subject and depends almost wholly on what the viewer is able to make of impressionistic details and broad outlines on the canvas.

The Gospels give us portraits of Jesus. Far too much has been omitted from the life of Jesus for the accounts to be considered photographs. The writers not only were selective in what they included; they also gave a particular interpretation of the person and work of Jesus, making no attempt to give a wholly objective recording of the facts. Verbal portraits always leave a lot to the imagination of the reader, and those in the Gospels are no exception. Each Gospel gives us a distinctive portrait of Jesus in which certain things are highlighted and others omitted.

One scholar has proposed the television sports replay as a model for what we find in the Gospels:

> In these replays the action can be dramatically slowed down so that one is able to see much more than one was able to see in the action as it

2. I am indebted for this comparison to Robert A. Guelich, "The Gospels: Portraits of Jesus and His Ministry," *Journal of the Evangelical Theological Society* 24 (1982): 117–25.

actually occurred. If one is given the full treatment—close-up, slow-action, forward-and-reverse, split-screen, the same scene from several perspectives, and with the verbal commentary and interpretation of an expert superimposed—one has a fair analogy of what the evangelists do. . . . One might add to the significance of the analogy by pointing out that the true significance of certain plays can only be known after the game is over.[3]

Most of the alleged discrepancies among the Gospels have resulted from an inaccurate understanding of the literary principles on which they are founded.

The Style of the Gospels

The most notable stylistic trait of the Gospels is their economy of words and details. This was nothing new, since it is also the norm for storytelling in the Old Testament. But the tendency is perhaps even more pronounced in the Gospels. As in the Old Testament stories, we find a preference for the brief unit, a relatively self-contained quality to the individual episodes, a prevailing realism, an impulse toward dialogue and dramatic techniques, and a simple, unembellished style.

Anyone who has tried his or her hand at writing a story will sense at once the skill with which the Gospel writers managed to select the significant detail that embodies the maximum meaning. In this kind of narrative artistry, what the writers omit is as important as what they include, and the Gospels are notable for their understated approach to the world-changing events they record. It is a tribute to their success that so few words can produce such a vivid impression in our imaginations.

Because of their prevailing brevity and conciseness, the Gospels combine simplicity and difficulty. Despite the surface simplicity, the individual units are often perplexing when we move from description to interpretation. Many passages tease us into trying to discover their significance without giving us the kind of help that would make that discovery easy. Yet the overall message of the Gospels is easily grasped.

Subtypes Within the Gospels

All of the Gospels share a reliance on certain subtypes or subgenres. Each of these has its governing ingredients and traits. Knowing the range of possibilities will help us make more sense of individual pas-

---

3. Donald A. Hagner, "Interpreting the Gospels: The Landscape and the Quest," *Journal of the Evangelical Theological Society* 24 (1981): 34.

sages when we come upon them. I should also note that my list of subtypes focuses on narrative units, leaving the material in discourses (including parables, sayings, and addresses) for treatment elsewhere.

Annunciation and Nativity Stories

The Gospels of Matthew and Luke begin with a series of stories that deal with events surrounding the birth of Jesus. Some of these are annunciation stories in which angels appear to people and make predictions about the birth of Jesus or related incidents. A feature of these stories is the inclusion of lyric poems embedded in the narrative. Nativity stories recount what happened when Jesus was actually born, including stories of his early infancy. Luke adds the boyhood story of Jesus in the temple at age twelve (2:41–52).

The main purpose of these stories is to accentuate the uniqueness of Jesus, to explain his significance, to validate the historical facts of the matter, to record the supernatural occurrences surrounding the events, and to document the fulfillment of Old Testament prophecies about the coming Messiah. The main literary feature of these stories is the excitement that they convey about the world-changing events that they narrate.

Calling or Vocation Stories

The Gospels contain a number of stories in which Jesus called people to follow him or to respond to a specific command. Such calling stories include (but are not limited to) the calling of the disciples. The four ingredients and corresponding questions to ask of the text are these:

1. The *characters* involved: who is called?
2. The *circumstances* in which the call occurs: where does the call of Jesus come to people?
3. The *nature* of the call: to what does Jesus call people?
4. The *response* to the call: what constitutes the right or wrong response to the call of Jesus?

In reading these stories, we should remember the basic narrative principle that characters in a story carry a burden of meaning larger than themselves. They are representatives of the human race generally. When Jesus calls a character in the Gospels, he also calls us.

This is a good place to note another feature of the Gospels. Usually when we read stories we identify with the protagonist or hero. In the Gospels, the one character with whom we do not identify in the sense of equating ourselves with him is Jesus. We identify with other characters. They are our substitutes and represent us as they respond to Jesus. Roland Frye has said that the characters in the Gospels

> are sketched with sure strokes, but not so fully as to preclude our iden-
> tifying ourselves with them. Their faces are never so completely drawn
> that we cannot place our own heads on their shoulders: we could be
> blind man, neighbor, parent, or Pharisee, and it can be instructive for us
> to assume each role in turn as we read.[4]

Recognition Stories

In recognition stories a character discovers who Jesus is. These stories dispense with plot conflict and keep the focus instead on the movement toward the character's moment of recognition or insight.

Two ingredients assume importance in these stories. One is the circumstances of the recognition, including the occasion, setting, and characters involved. The important question here is *how* the circumstances lead to the recognition. The second major element is the precise nature of *what* a character comes to recognize about Jesus. As readers we identify with characters in these stories. Their moment of epiphany is one that we share with them.

These stories contribute in a particularly direct way to the central purpose of the Gospels, which is to explain the person and work of Christ. It is natural to focus, therefore, on what these stories tell us about Jesus.

Witness Stories

In witness or testimony stories, either Jesus or another character testifies about who Jesus is or what he has done. These stories are similar to recognition stories, but instead of moving toward a moment of recognition, we listen to someone's proclamation about Jesus.

Witness stories usually consist of three main ingredients. We can phrase them as three questions:

1. *Who?* (The witness.)
2. *What?* (The testimony.)
3. *Why?* (The proof, which might include circumstances.)

When the witness is Jesus himself, the focus is on the second of these elements rather than the third. Because the question of evidence is

---

4. Roland Frye, "The Jesus of the Gospels: Approaches Through Narrative Structure," in *From Faith to Faith: Essays in Honor of Donald G. Miller, on His Seventieth Birthday*, ed. Dikran Y. Hadidian, Pittsburgh Theological Monographs, no. 31 (Pittsburgh: Pickwick, 1979), p. 79.

important in these stories, it is usually profitable to explore the logic between the claim that is made about Jesus and the evidence on which it is based.

Encounter Stories

In his most characteristic pose in the Gospels, Jesus is encountering a character or a group. The story of Zacchaeus (Luke 19:1–10) shows the genre on a small scale, the story of the Samaritan woman (John 4:1–42) on a grand scale. These stories should be approached as dramas. We can divide them into scenes and speeches. The essential action usually consists of dialogue rather than external events.

Encounter stories follow a predictable rhythm of movement. They have a firm progression and wholeness. They begin when either Jesus or another character initiates the encounter. Jesus asks the Samaritan woman for a drink, for example, and tells Zacchaeus that he plans to stay overnight at his house. Once the encounter has been initiated, we can trace the progress of the dialogue toward its goal. In retrospect, at least, we can identify the purpose or goal toward which Jesus builds the encounter. Encounter stories are strongly goal-oriented, being essentially quest stories.

At the end, the person encountered either accepts or rejects the claim that Jesus has made on his or her life. The outcome of these stories is crucial. The people who are encountered by Jesus in effect undergo a test that they either pass or fail.

As elsewhere in the Gospels, we should regard the people who encounter Jesus as representative of people generally. The premise in these stories is that everyone must face the claims of Jesus. Encounter stories are parables of the human condition and of how Jesus speaks to that condition.

Conflict or Controversy Stories

Conflict stories are the prototypical Gospel story—most like ordinary stories and also among the most numerous in the Gospels. These stories pit Jesus against an opposing person or group. They give the Gospels much of their color and excitement, and they move the overall action inexorably toward the eventual trial and death of Jesus.

Jesus is always the protagonist in a conflict story, regardless of whether he or his opponents originate the conflict. We need to identify the antagonists or villains in such a story, as well as the reason for their antagonism against Jesus and the exact means by which they try to trap or defeat Jesus.

As for the progress of the action, we can usually plot the steps by which the conflict between Jesus and his opponents proceeds. In particular, we can note Jesus' strategies of defense and offense or coun-terattack. These stories are built on a back-and-forth rhythm in which Jesus always gets the advantage. We also need to interpret how the conflict is finally resolved, and determine the lesson we are intended to learn from this resolution.

Pronouncement Stories

One of the distinctive subtypes in the Gospels is the pronouncement story. This is a brief story in which an event in Jesus' life is linked with a memorable saying or proverb by Jesus. Usually the event leads up to and culminates in the saying. The saying is embedded in the narrative in such a way that the two are remembered together.

The important principle in pronouncement stories is that the story is related to the saying as a stimulus is related to a response. The saying either interprets or illustrates the event. The interpretation of such a story will in large part be an exploration of how the two parts correlate. Pronouncement stories can themselves be subdivided into six categories—stories of correction, objection, commendation, quest, test, and inquiry.[5]

Pronouncement stories are a Gospel hallmark. In fact, memorable sayings are often an ingredient in other Gospel subtypes (especially conflict stories), resulting in what might be called hybrid forms.

Miracle Stories

Another form that we especially associate with the Gospels is the miracle story. The typical structure of a miracle story is this:

1. A need is established.
2. Jesus' help is sought.
3. The person in need (or his acquaintances) expresses faith or obedience.
4. Jesus performs a miracle.
5. Characters in the story respond to the miracle and/or to Jesus.

A given miracle story might omit one or more of these elements.

There is a remarkable variety in the miracle stories. Some are skel-etal outlines of what happened, while others are narrated in leisurely and full detail. Sometimes the miracle is the center of attention, while at other times it is subsidiary to another issue (thereby making the

5. For more on these classifications, see Robert C. Tannehill, "Attitudinal Shift in Synoptic Pronouncement Stories," in *Orientation by Disorientation: Studies in Literary Criticism and Biblical Literary Criticism Presented in Honor of William A. Beardslee*, ed. Richard A. Spencer, Pittsburgh Theological Monographs, no. 35 (Pittsburgh: Pickwick, 1980), p. 184.

story a hybrid). Sometimes the physical miracle attests the power of Jesus, while on other occasions the miracle takes on a symbolic meaning or is told in such a way as to teach a lesson (about faith, for example).

Passion Stories

The events surrounding the trial, death, and resurrection of Jesus form the climax of all four Gospels. If we count chapters, the percentages of each Gospel devoted to the passion of Jesus are as follows: Matthew, 29; Mark, 38; Luke, 25; and John, 38. Increasing specificity of detail characterizes the storytelling method as the writers reach the passion account. Obviously this is what the Gospel writers regarded as most important in their stories.

If we view the four passion stories as a composite whole, we can further subdivide them into discernible stories: arrival in Jerusalem, the Passover and the upper room, suffering in Gethsemane, arrest, trial, crucifixion, burial, resurrection, and postresurrection appearances. Here, too, we find the convergence of both tragedy and comedy as the Gospels move through suffering to their happy ending.

Hybrid Stories

The narrative genres I have discussed often converge in individual stories. When they do, it is possible to discuss stories in terms of two or more of these types. Miracle stories often become recognition stories as well. Memorable sayings by Jesus are so customary in the Gospel narratives that the criteria of the pronouncement story are often relevant to stories that overall would be classified as something else. When Jesus called his followers, the call often included a miraculous element, and the story accordingly has the ingredients of both a calling story and a miracle story. Despite the combination of elements in these hybrid stories, however, the way in which the writer handles the story often makes one of the story types the dominant element.

The Gospel of John

The dominant pattern of the Gospels is story or narrative, but this becomes obscured when we read them piecemeal. The full narrative sweep of a Gospel dawns on us only when we read it continuously the way we read a short story or novel. To illustrate the narrative features of a Gospel, I have selected the most literary Gospel, the Gospel of John.[6]

6. Among book-length literary analyses of individual Gospels, I recommend David Rhoads and Donald Michie's book *Mark as Story: An Introduction to the Narrative of a Gospel* (Philadelphia: Fortress, 1982).

A narrative approach to a Gospel will concern itself, among other things, with the overall unity and design of the work. The impact of any long narrative depends in part on the overriding structure that the writer is able to impose on the details. The Gospel of John is built on several unifying principles that span the book.

Structure and Unity

In its general outline, the book follows the chronology of the protagonist's public career. It thus begins with an account of Jesus' divine origin. It then proceeds through the preparatory ministry of John the Baptist, the early events of Jesus' public ministry, some main incidents of his career as an itinerant religious teacher, and finally his trial, death, and resurrection. This is clearly a story with a beginning, middle, and end.

In fact, the self-conscious shaping by Jesus of his own life has all the shapeliness of a carefully constructed story. At every stage it is evident that Jesus was controlling his life according to a plan. The climax toward which his entire life was slanted was his death and resurrection. This movement toward a climax can be traced through the successive references to the "hour" of Jesus, an allusion to the time of his death and resurrection.

Early in the book there are references to the fact that Jesus' hour has not yet come (2:4; 7:30; 8:20). We also encounter statements that "the hour is coming" (4:21; 5:28). Late in the narrative there are reminders that Christ's hour has definitely arrived (12:23; 31:1; 17:1). As the final confrontation with the Jews approaches, Jesus begins to speak more openly of his coming death, and in his last public discourse he defines his whole purpose on earth as being his death as the Savior of the world (12:20–36).

Another element of narrative structure is the progressive intensification of plot conflict and a corresponding movement toward the climax of the story. The writer begins his story with events that evoked no conflict (the miracle at Cana, the discourses with Nicodemus and the Samaritan woman, the healing of the official's son), and then moves to acts of Jesus that elicited extreme conflict (the healing on the sabbath, the argument over Christ's claims to be the bread of life, the controversy at the Feast of Tabernacles, and so forth). Finally there is the overt conspiracy to kill Jesus and at last the crucifixion itself.

The only exception to this pattern of increasing hostility is the cleansing of the temple (2:13–16), a scene of violent conflict that appears early and serves the narrative function of foreshadowing the eventual struggle between Jesus and the Jews and the ultimate victory of Jesus in this struggle. We might note, too, that in the cleansing of the temple Jesus initiates the conflict, whereas later chapters about the ongoing struggle feature the antagonism of the Jews against Jesus.

The Gospel of John is also structured on the principle of expansion followed by constriction. The action begins with an account of Jesus' relations with a small circle of believers, including John the Baptist, the disciples he called to follow him, and his family and friends, seen with Jesus at the wedding of an acquaintance in Cana. From this intimate circle of friends, Jesus' public ministry quickly expands throughout Palestine and encompasses huge crowds of people, as Jesus becomes one of the most talked-about public figures of his time. As the conspiracy to kill Jesus grows, his contacts again become constricted. During the last week of his life, he spends his time with the disciples, and his postresurrection appearances likewise involve the small inner circle of friends.

Yet another aspect of the structural unity of the Gospel of John is the overriding conflict between belief and unbelief. Keeping Jesus always in the center of the action, the writer presents a series of responses by people who come into contact with the protagonist. At root, these responses show either belief or unbelief in the saving work of Jesus. In John's Gospel, the unbelief is concentrated in "the Jews," that is, the religious leaders.

Many individual episodes are specifically tied to this ongoing struggle, which is based on Jesus' clash with his social and religious environment. In the words of G. Wilson Knight, the Gospel pictures Jesus "silhouetted against a world of formalized religion, hypocrisy, envy, evil and suffering."[7] The writer's purpose in presenting this conflict between belief and unbelief is to instill belief in the reader, as he makes clear at the end of the book: "Now Jesus did many other signs in the presence of the disciples, which are not written in this book; but these are written that you may believe that Jesus is the Christ, the Son of God, and that believing you may have life in his name" (20:30–31).

Patterns

John's skill in organizing the material is evident not only in his management of the overall narrative structure but also in his construction of smaller units. One of these elements of design consists of combining an event that involves Jesus with a discourse that interprets the meaning of the event. Typical examples include Jesus' request for a drink from the Samaritan woman followed by his statements about the water of life (chap. 4), the healing on the sabbath linked to Christ's words about his divine authority (chap. 5), the feeding of the five thou-

---

7. G. Wilson Knight, *The Christian Renaissance* (New York: Norton, 1962), p. 169.

sand related to the discourse on the bread of life (chap. 6), and the raising of Lazarus accompanied by Jesus' remarks about his being the resurrection and the life (chap. 11).

An elaboration of this narrative technique is the linking of a single discourse to two events. For example, the discourse on Christ as the light of the world (chap. 8) is flanked by references to attendance at the Feast of Tabernacles, where the burning of huge torches was part of the ritual (chap. 7), and the giving of sight to the blind man (chap. 9). The same pattern occurs with the discourse on the bread of heaven, which is placed in the context of both the Passover and the feeding of the five thousand (chap. 6).

Yet another variation of this pattern is the relation of a single event to two discourses. For example, the healing of the blind man (chap. 9) illustrates Jesus' preceding discourse about the light of the world (chap. 8), while the expulsion of the healed man from the synagogue leads immediately into Jesus' discourse about the good shepherd and bad shepherds (chap. 10). The author's sensitivity to symbolism is obvious in all this, since the events that he narrates are external symbols of the theological truths that Christ proclaims in his accompanying discourses.

A similar type of narrative pattern that underlies a number of individual episodes is the motif of the misunderstood statement. These dramas in miniature unfold in three stages: Jesus makes a pronouncement, a bystander expresses a misunderstanding of the utterance, and Jesus proceeds to explain the meaning of his original statement. This narrative pattern occurs no fewer than nine times in the book.[8] Usually the misunderstanding arises when Jesus' statement calls for a figurative or symbolic interpretation and is given a literal meaning by the bystander, a fact whose significance for interpreting the Gospel should not be overlooked.

The fourth Gospel also makes use of number patterns in a manner similar to that which pervades the Book of Revelation. Patterns of three are prominent. The narrator records three Passovers and three other feasts that Jesus attended. Early in the book John the Baptist three times witnesses to Christ's messiahship. Late in the narrative Jesus is three times condemned. He also speaks three times from the cross. There are three denials by Peter and three stages in Christ's restoration of Peter.

There is a similar use of the number seven. The writer structures the central part of his narrative around seven great miracles or "signs"

8. The passages are as follows: 3:3–8; 4:10–15; 4:31–38; 6:47–58; 7:33–36; 8:21–30; 8:31–47; 8:56–58; 11:11–15. The pattern appears with slight modification in 2:17–22.

that Jesus performed. The list includes turning the water into wine (2:1–11), the healing of the official's son (4:46–54), the cure of the paralytic (5:1–18), the feeding of the five thousand (6:5–13), walking on the water (6:16–21), the healing of the blind man (9:1–7), and the raising of Lazarus (11:1–44).

Equally important is the pattern of seven statements by Jesus beginning with the formula *I am* and followed by a metaphoric description of Jesus' person and work: the bread of life (6:35), the light of the world (8:12), the door of the sheep (10:7), the good shepherd (10:11), the resurrection and the life (11:25), the way, the truth, and the life (14:6), and the true vine (15:1). As the book unfolds there is also a sevenfold witness to Christ: the witness of the Father (5:37; 8:18), of the Son (8:14; 18:37), of Christ's works (5:36; 10:25), of Scripture (5:39–46), of John the Baptist (1:7; 5:35), of the disciples (15:27; 19:35), and of the Spirit (15:26; 16:14).

The Flow of the Story

A literary approach to the Gospels is concerned not only with the elements of narrative pattern and design but also with the sequential unfolding of the story. The progress of the story from beginning to end—the sequential ordering of the material—is of prime importance if we read the book as a story. The following survey of the Gospel of John thus attempts to reconstruct the linear development of the story as we actually read the book.

John begins his story with a lyric prologue (1:1–18). The narrative function is to introduce the reader to the protagonist or hero of the story. He is introduced to us as the incarnate Christ, both divine and human, both heavenly and earthly. Two chief functions are ascribed to Christ in the prologue: he is the revelation of God to people, and he is the bringer of spiritual life.

The prologue also introduces some stylistic traits that will permeate the story to follow. Already we see a reliance on symbol and metaphor as the form through which the nature of God's unprecedented disclosure in Christ is conveyed. Thus Christ is presented as "the Word" and as "the light" that "shines in the darkness" and "enlightens every man." We are also introduced to the great conflicts around which the story will be built—conflicts between light and darkness, Christ's being in the world and yet rejected by the world, his coming to his own home and not being received there.

The remainder of the first chapter is devoted to a few brief narratives that introduce us to the protagonist by showing his impact on other people. One of these people is John the Baptist, who regards his successful ministry as only the prelude to the even greater ministry of the coming Messiah (1:19–34). Already as we read we can see that the essential purpose of the story will be to portray, explain, and exalt the central character. This reaches its early climax in the story of Christ's baptism, which is accompanied by the supernatural sign of the descent of the Spirit in the form of a dove (1:29–34).

These early witness and recognition stories are followed by several calling or vocation stories (1:35–51). Here, too, the protagonist is characterized by the loyalty and worship that he elicits from his followers. Dialogue is the basic mode of these stories, as we hear voices calling, responding, and explaining. The effect is to place us as participants and spectators of the world-changing events that make up the essential material of the Gospels.

Variety of episode is necessary to any good story. Monotony dulls the effect. After viewing the kaleidoscope of brief scenes and characters that makes up chapter 1, we enter a slower-paced world in chapter 2, which is devoted to just two events, the miracle at Cana and the cleansing of the temple. Having shown the protagonist indirectly by dramatizing how he influences those around him, the writer now moves to a more direct presentation of Jesus in action.

The miracle of turning water into wine (2:1–11) is the first of seven great miracles that Jesus performs in the Gospel of John. In terms of storytelling technique, John here draws upon his staple—a combination of summarized narrative (in which the writer tells us what happened) and dramatized dialogue. This early episode belongs to the familiar archetype of the initiation, as the author emphasizes that it was "the first of his signs" (v. 11).

The precise term *sign* is important in this Gospel. John uses the term to draw attention to the significance inherent in Jesus' miracles. They are not simply factual events or physical phenomena but symbols of spiritual reality. This fusion of event and symbolic meaning is one of the most distinctive features of John's Gospel. It is an essentially literary approach in which truth is imaged in concrete form.

What meaning, then, did this great sign embody? This is an interpretive question that the Gospel of John continuously requires us to answer. John himself makes one meaning explicit when he states that Christ's miracle "manifested his glory" in such a way that "his disciples believed in him" (v. 11). But even when the narrator tells us the truth about his great symbols, he does not necessarily tell us the whole truth.

Another meaning is implicit in this parabolic miracle of Jesus. The six stone jars contained water that was used for the ceremonial rituals that would have accompanied a Jewish wedding. By turning this water into wine, Jesus was announcing, through a symbolic act, that he had come to fulfill and supersede the ceremonial laws of Old Testament religion. In the background of the episode is another biblical archetype, the messianic banquet, in which the kingdom of God is compared to a feast. The quantity of water changed to wine is symbolic of the abundance of the messianic banquet, a fact that the narrator himself makes explicit by emphasizing that each of the jars held "twenty or thirty gallons" (v. 6).

As we conclude this early event in the story, then, we can rest assured that as readers we have been initiated into the storyteller's essential method of narration. We now know that his story exists to tell us the truth about the protagonist, Jesus. Much of the meaning of the story, moreover, will be embodied in symbolic images and events. The main intent of the story (to acquaint the reader with the person and work of Christ) will be clear—in fact, the narrator can be trusted to provide interpretive signposts to guide us. But much of the meaning of the story will depend on our ability to see deeper meanings in the surface details. Those meanings, moreover, will have a lot to do with Christ's fulfillment of Old Testament foreshadowings.

Up to this point in the narrative, Jesus has been shown in his relations with a small circle of friends and relatives. With the episode of the cleansing of the temple (2:13–25), the scope of the action broadens as Jesus enters the public spotlight. Here is the first conflict or controversy story in a Gospel that will rely heavily on this form. Like many events in the Gospels, this one is narrated with vivid and dramatic detail. It is as though we are witnessing the event in person or on television.

As elsewhere in the Gospels, we are asked to interpret the meaning of the event in terms of the mission of Christ. In cleansing the temple, Christ asserts his authority by challenging the religious establishment of his day. The event also introduces a note of revolution into the story as Christ uses physical force to single-handedly drive the moneychangers out of the temple. This is not a private campaign but a messianic gesture in which God himself enters his temple with divine authority to cleanse it. In this episode we also find the first misunderstood statement of Jesus when he utters the enigmatic statement, "Destroy this temple, and in three days I will raise it up" (2:19).

Jesus' dialogue with Nicodemus about the new birth (3:1–15) is typical of the self-contained nature of the narrative pieces that the Gospel writers compiled as they told their stories of Jesus. The basic model of action is threefold: a character enters the life of Jesus, encounters the claims of Jesus, and then drops out of the story. Dialogue is the means of encounter in these stories.

In the story of Nicodemus we find Jesus in a new role in the Gospel of John, the role of teacher. The story itself is an encounter story built around another of Jesus' misunderstood utterances. Nicodemus misinterprets Jesus' statement that "unless one is born anew, he cannot see the kingdom of God" (3:3) when he interprets the statement literally. He asks, "How can a man be born when he is old? Can he enter a second time into his mother's womb and be born?" (3:4). Jesus responds by interpreting his original statement as referring to a spiritual birth (3:6–8). This dialogue about spiritual birth becomes linked to the overriding plot of John's Gospel when Jesus defines the new birth in terms of belief: "that whoever believes in [me] may have eternal life" (3:15).

Several common strategies of the Gospels converge in an episode like the story of Nicodemus. The Gospels are a series of epiphanies (revelations or disclosures leading to spiritual insight) in which we as readers share a character's gradual movement toward perception regarding Jesus. This pattern corresponds to what we can infer about the formation of the Gospels: they are composed of units that grew up around the disciples' early (oral) proclamation about Jesus. No doubt the stories about Jesus that were used most in the preaching of the disciples were those that could most easily be used to teach the basic outlines of the Christian faith.

The writers who compiled the stories and put them into the collections known as the Gospels molded their material according to their purposes. They kept their history about Jesus in a clearly discernible interpretive framework. This is well illustrated when the account of Christ's discussion with Nicodemus is followed by the narrator's commentary that elaborates the statements made by Jesus (3:16–21). These verses, beginning with the famous statement that "God so loved the world that he gave his only Son, that whoever believes in him should not perish but have eternal life," are both theological teaching and the writer's personal testimony. The Gospels were written by people who had been transformed by their experience with Christ and who wanted others to share the same experience.

Jesus' conversation with the Samaritan woman at the well (4:1–30) is one of the most famous of the elaborated Gospel stories. It is the classic encounter story in the Gospels. As with other encounter stories, this one is a drama in miniature. The physical stage is set with realistic details: "So he came to a city of Samaria. . . . Jacob's well was there, and so Jesus, wearied as he was with his journey, sat down beside the well. It was about the sixth hour." Dialogue carries the essential meaning of the encounter that follows. As so often is true in the Gospels, drama is the mode of presentation.

The story is also a masterpiece of narrative art. Encounter stories

48   **Words of Life**

are essentially quest stories in which Jesus initiates a conversation
and slants it toward the goal of bringing a person to belief. The sense
of progression toward the goal is overpowering in this story as we
trace the back-and-forth movement between the two speakers. It is a
classic case of one thing leading to the next. The plot has the usual
beginning-middle-end shapeliness that we associate with well-made
stories. It begins with Jesus' apparently casual request for a drink of
water. It proceeds to Christ's progressive self-disclosure as the prom-
ised Messiah about whom the woman herself speaks. The story ends
with the woman's belief and testimony. The story even has the moment of reversal that Aristotle liked in stories: the woman thinks to
dismiss the religious claims that Jesus has just made with the comment that "when [Messiah] comes, he will show us all things" (4:25),
but Jesus shocks her by saying, "I who speak to you am he" (4:26).[9]

The characterization of the Samaritan woman also makes the story
memorable. She is the archetypal outcast who comes to the well at
noon when no one else would be present. She is a moral drifter, having
had five divorces and now living with a lover. When the subject turns
to religion, she tries to evade the real issue by raising a point of theological dispute: "Our fathers worshiped on this mountain and you
say that in Jerusalem is the place where men ought to worship" (4:20).
The Gospels are rich in recognizable human experience. We have all
met the Samaritan woman in the routine of our lives. In fact, we can
see much of ourselves in her.

The story of Jesus and the Samaritan woman epitomizes the Gospel
as a literary form. If we are looking for the standard ingredients of the
Gospel, we can find them here: the focus on Jesus as protagonist, the
travel motif, the prominence of nature as a setting for the action,
realism of description, the prominence of dialogue, the presence of
archetypal symbols (in this case, water as a symbol of eternal life), a
miraculous element (Jesus knows the woman's entire marital history
without having met her before), the presence of mysterious sayings by
Jesus (e.g., "whoever drinks of the water that I shall give him will
never thirst"), a preoccupation with spiritual salvation as the central
issue, and a crowd of onlookers drawn into the action.

The individual stories that make up the Gospels exist on a continuum based on length or shortness. The story of the Samaritan woman
is an embellished story, told in a leisurely pace and filled out with
realistic description and dialogue. But this literary impulse is mingled

9. I mention Aristotle by design: his *Poetics* remains the definitive starting point
on the subject of plot in stories and is an excellent source of terms for discussing the
Gospels.

with the starkest documentary impulse to record the facts and no more. This is well illustrated by the fragment that immediately follows the drama at the well of Jacob:

> After the two days he departed to Galilee. For Jesus himself testified that a prophet has no honor in his own country. So when he came to Galilee, the Galileans welcomed him, having seen all that he had done in Jerusalem at the feast, for they too had gone to the feast. [4:43–45]

Such fragments serve as reminders that the degree of literary intention in the Gospels varies.

The healing of the official's son (4:46–54) is another miracle story. We find the usual ingredients: a need established, the help of Jesus sought, an expression of faith, the performance of a miracle, and a response from those involved in the miracle. In terms of the bigger movement of the Gospel as a whole, a miracle story such as this shows Christ's supernatural power, his compassion for the physical needs of people, and the way in which those who realized Christ's divine power were brought to belief.

The healing of the paralytic man at Bethesda on the sabbath (chap. 5) is a miracle story on the grand scale. Although it is a healing story like the episode preceding it, the differences between the two miracles show the narrative principle of variety that is almost always at work in the Gospels. In the place of a brief narrative, we have an elaborated story. Whereas the healing of the official's son led to belief, this miracle ends in conflict with the Pharisees over the issue of whether the healing had violated the law about keeping the sabbath and over Christ's claims of authority (5:10–18). In the healing of the official's son, the account of the miracle was followed by a one-sentence summary of the belief of those who witnessed the miracle. Here the description of the miracle is accompanied by the extended discourse of Jesus about his divine authority (5:19–47). This fusion of act and discourse, event and spiritual significance, is of course a chief differentiating feature of John's Gospel. In this instance, Jesus' discourse is devoted to his self-characterization, as he explains who he is. The frequent self-characterization of the protagonist is one of the things that makes the Gospels unique as stories.

The miraculous feeding of five thousand people (6:1–14) perpetuates the narrative pattern of variety in unity. The basic elements of the miracle story persist, but there are changes as well. The miracle itself involves sustaining life instead of healing disease. It encompasses a huge crowd of people; earlier miracles involved individuals. Along with the differences is an element of sameness, as the story winds its way back at the end to the overriding plot of the Gospel as a whole, the struggle between belief and unbelief: "When the people saw the sign which he had done, they said, 'This is indeed the prophet who is to come into the world!' " (6:14).

In keeping with the basic narrative strategy in the Gospel of John, the miracle of the feeding of the crowd is a sign that reaches its culmination in an interpretive discourse, in this case Jesus' discourse on his status as the bread of life (6:22–40). The Gospel of John is famous for its symbolism, and here is a prime example. The physical image of bread becomes symbolic of a spiritual reality. The very rhetoric that Jesus uses in talking about bread shows this mingling of the physical and the spiritual: "food which endures to eternal life (v. 27), "the true bread from heaven" (v. 32), "the bread of life" (v. 35), "the living bread which came down from heaven" (v. 51). Here, truly, the physical becomes transformed into something more than physical.

Many of the episodes in John's Gospel begin with narration of an event and then expand by showing the repercussions of the initial stimulus. The story we have just considered is typical. It begins with a miracle, followed by a discourse in which Jesus elaborates the physical miracle, transforming it into a spiritual symbol. The discourse, in turn, generates disagreement, first among the Jews (6:41–59) and then among the disciples (6:60–71). Belief versus unbelief continues to hold center stage as the Gospel unfolds.

In summary, the long sixth chapter illustrates the typical structure of the embellished stories found in the Gospels. The storyteller's impulse in these stories is to linger on an event, not simply to give the bare outline. In the center of the action are the person and work of Jesus. The story begins with an event that is then elaborated in a discourse. Then both become transmuted into a conflict between belief and unbelief.

The Gospels use two chief means of characterizing the protagonist. One is Jesus' self-characterization through deed and word. The other is the response of others to Jesus' claims about himself. The account of Christ's appearance at the Feast of Tabernacles (chap. 7) illustrates the interplay between these two types of characterization as we witness a bewildering variety of responses to Jesus' claims about himself. One response is the hostility of the Jewish leaders. In keeping with the plot structure of increasing antagonism against Jesus, the earlier intellectual debate now intensifies into a conspiracy to kill Jesus (7:1, 25), and even an unsuccessful attempt to arrest him (v. 32). The sheer danger and adventure of the story should not escape us as we read the Gospels.

Another response of people is uncertainty about the claims of Jesus:

"And there was much muttering about him among the people. While some said, 'He is a good man,' others said, 'No, he is leading the people astray' " (7:12). A third response is belief in Jesus as Savior, as evidenced by the report that "many of the people believed in him" (7:31). Behind this pattern of varied response is the clear call of Jesus for people to believe in him: "If any one thirst, let him come to me and drink" (v. 37). Like so many other chapters in the Gospels, this one is full of voices—voices arguing and voices expressing perplexity, hostility, and belief.

Debate and conflict also govern the next chapter (8), in which Jesus defends his claims against the Pharisees. The chapter begins with the Pharisees placing a woman caught in adultery in front of Jesus "to test him, that they might have some charge to bring against him" (8:6). It ends with the Jews taking up stones to throw at Jesus (v. 59). Sandwiched between these two conflicts is a prolonged altercation between Jesus and the Pharisees. It should be obvious how much is lost if we do not approach the Gospels as stories. They are fast-paced and action-filled, having much more in common with a novel or a television drama than a sermon.

Earlier I called the Gospel of John the most literary of the Gospels. This claim is not based only on John's poetic sensitivity to image and symbol. It also stems from John's tendency to work with relatively long episodes and to embellish them with literary technique. John is rarely content simply to record what happened. He recreates events in such a way as to tell us how things happened so we can relive them.

The story of the healing of the man born blind (chap. 9) illustrates to perfection this literary inclination.[10] The story is conceived dramatically, with virtually all the action embodied in the form of dialogue among various characters. The action shifts from scene to scene in a way that makes us feel as though we are watching it on television. The drama is shot through with realism, humor, and controversy. It is as recognizably chaotic as a committee meeting that has gotten out of control.

To lend purpose and design to the story, John includes an interpretive framework at the outset. The disciples ask Jesus, "Rabbi, who sinned, this man or his parents, that he was born blind?" (9:2). Jesus challenges their conventional way of thinking by replying that the man's blindness was not the result of sin but that "the works of God

10. For a fuller explication than I attempt here, and as an excellent illustration of the type of literary analysis to which the Gospels lend themselves, I commend James L. Resseguie's essay "John 9: A Literary-Critical Analysis," in *Literary Interpretations of Biblical Narratives, Volume II*, ed. Kenneth R. R. Gros Louis (Nashville: Abingdon, 1982), pp. 295–303.

might be made manifest in him" (v. 3). The miracle that follows, then, will be another of the revealing signs of John's Gospel, manifesting the power and compassion of God. The sign itself is a thoroughly physical event, as Jesus "spat on the ground and made clay of the spittle and anointed the man's eyes with the clay" (v. 6).

The elaboration of the miraculous sign follows a now familiar pattern. The actual miracle begins an ever-widening series of ripples in the community. True to life, the first people to hear of the miracle are the healed man's neighbors (vv. 8–12). From the neighborhood the action moves to the religious leaders (vv. 13–34), who finally cast the man out of the synagogue. There is humor as well as pathos in the episode, with the Pharisees inflexibly denying the obvious healing of the man and the equally obvious divine power of Jesus. This is a good episode with which to note, therefore, the pervasive satiric element in the Gospels. Satire is the exposure, through ridicule or rebuke, of human vice or folly. In the events of the Gospels, as well as the parables and discourses of Jesus, there is continuous satire, usually directed against the Jewish religious leaders.[11]

At its end, the story of the healing of the blind man winds its way back to the unifying plot conflict of the Gospel as a whole. It is the conflict between belief and unbelief. After Jesus seeks out the man who has just been thrust out of the synagogue, the man believes and worships Jesus (vv. 35–38), while the Pharisees who witness this scene of belief remain the archetypal refusers of festivity (vv. 39–41). Jesus charges them with blindness, a concluding reminder that this is another episode in John's Gospel that is unified around a controlling image that symbolizes the spiritual meaning of the main event.

The culminating belief of the man who was healed shows how strongly oriented toward a goal the individual stories of the Gospels are. There is an incipient quest motif underlying most episodes in the Gospels. Jesus initiates action and utters discourses with a view to bringing people to a response. Knowing that this is how the episodes are structured, we are in a better position to organize the movement and details of a Gospel story around its appointed goal. Beginning at the end is usually a helpful way of analyzing a Gospel story.

The organizing pattern of John's Gospel is to combine events with accompanying discourses that seize upon a central image from the event. Jesus' famous discourse about his being the good shepherd

11. For more on satire in the New Testament, see chapter 14 of my companion volume to this book, *Words of Delight: A Literary Introduction to the Bible* (Grand Rapids: Baker, 1987). On the element of humor in the Gospels that is usually overlooked, the classic source is Elton Trueblood, *The Humor of Christ* (New York: Harper and Row, 1964).

(10:1–21) perpetuates this pattern. The comments about the ignoble shepherds who are motivated by greed and who abandon their sheep cast a retrospective look at the behavior of the Pharisees who rejected the healed man. The care of the good shepherd described in the discourse likewise explains the actions of Jesus in his dealings with the healed man.

The importance of the discourse about the good shepherd reaches out to other contexts as well. The discourse comes in the middle of John's Gospel, for example, and by summarizing the redemptive life of Jesus it sounds the keynote for the entire Gospel. Within the larger context of the Bible as a whole, the discourse climaxes the tradition of pastoral literature in which religious issues are portrayed metaphorically in terms of shepherds and sheep (see, for example, Ezek. 34).

The next episode, the account of Jesus' appearance at the Feast of Dedication (10:22–42), parallels the earlier appearance at the Feast of Tabernacles (chap. 7). In fact, John refers to Jesus' attendance at six Jewish religious festivals. As a narrative principle, repetition of any type functions as a device of disclosure by which a storyteller signals what is important in the story. In keeping with John's strategy of attaching symbolic meanings to events, it is not hard to see the importance of Jesus' attendance at Jewish religious festivals. He is the fulfillment of Old Testament ceremonial laws and rituals. Not surprisingly, Jesus' attendance at these events generates controversy and conflict, as well as occasional belief.

The raising of Lazarus from the grave, coming near the middle of the Gospel of John, is a climactic episode. It is accordingly told in full circumstantial detail. To give the story a sense of unity and purpose from the beginning, John provides an interpretive framework at the outset: Jesus announces to his disciples that the death of Lazarus "is for the glory of God, so that the Son of God may be glorified by means of it" (11:4). Here, in fact, is the hidden agenda of all the Gospels. In terms of narrative classification, the Gospels are admiration stories in which the selection of material and storytelling technique are designed to exalt the hero of the story.

John's Gospel puts us in touch with a number of archetypes, such as light and darkness, water and bread, sight and blindness. The controlling archetype in the story of Lazarus is the death-rebirth pattern. It is combined with another common motif of John's Gospel, the misunderstood statement of Jesus. When Jesus tells his disciples that "our friend Lazarus has fallen asleep, but I go to awake him out of sleep" (v. 11), the disciples' perplexed response shows that for them the remark is a puzzle requiring a solution (vv. 12–16).

The story itself, in fact, is structured like a suspense story. First

Jesus delays his trip to Bethany for two days. His mysterious comments that Lazarus is only sleeping likewise seem to raise doubt that
he plans to do anything about the death. As Jesus approaches the
village, the friends and relatives of Lazarus come out to meet Jesus.
Instead of moving quickly to the miracle, John takes time to record
the conversations of Jesus with both Martha (vv. 20–27) and Mary (vv.
28–34). Then we picture the grief of Jesus and the responses it elicits
from onlookers (vv. 35–37).

The drama at the grave site is similarly suspenseful. Jesus commands that the stone be taken away, but having done so he has to
contend with Martha's objection that the body has begun to decom-
pose. After the stone is removed from the grave, Jesus prays to his
heavenly Father and cries out with a loud voice, "Lazarus, come out."
Then, almost beyond belief, we watch as "the dead man came out, his
hands and feet bound with bandages, and his face wrapped with a
cloth" (v. 44). As elsewhere in the Gospels, we have been participants
in an awe-inspiring event.

Individual episodes like this have a double allegiance. They are first
of all stories in themselves, built on a principle of beginning-middle-
end. But they are also building blocks in the overall edifice of the
Gospel. The Gospels adhere to the time-honored principles of good
composition: unity, coherence, and emphasis.

The story of the raising of Lazarus contributes in exactly this way
to the bigger story of John's Gospel. As elsewhere, a physical event
becomes symbolic of a spiritual reality. Usually this transformation
is explained in a discourse of Jesus, and this is true here as Jesus tells
Martha, "I am the resurrection and the life" (v. 25). Here, too, is one
of seven "I am" self-characterizations of Jesus around which John
builds his Gospel. As with the previous great signs recorded in the
Gospel, Jesus' raising of Lazarus generates resistance from the religious authorities (vv. 45–57).

In keeping with his practice of narrative variety, John follows the
embellished story of Lazarus with two brief narrative fragments. One
is the story of Mary of Bethany's anointing of Jesus (12:1–8). Mary's
act is a symbolic gesture, capturing as with a camera click the leading
Gospel theme of the supreme worthiness of Jesus. The episode also
reenacts the usual narrative pattern of event leading to conflict, as
Judas Iscariot and Jesus disagree on the appropriateness of the anointing (vv. 4–8). From another perspective, the contrast is between the
responses of Mary and Judas to the person of Jesus.

The triumphal entry into Jerusalem (12:12–19) is another simple
narrative. We might note that a Gospel writer's choice of whether to
use simple or embellished narrative does not depend on the significance of an event in the life of Jesus. The Gospel of Luke, for example,

treats the same event in much more detail. The decision regarding the length of an episode seems to have been a storyteller's decision rather than a theologian's. John uses the event of the triumphal entry to embody two themes—the imperfect understanding that the disciples had of the event until after Christ's glorification (vv. 14–16) and the popularity that Jesus enjoyed with the crowd at the height of his earthly career (vv. 17–19). The latter motif is continued in the ensuing narrative fragment about the Greeks who came to hear Jesus (vv. 20–22).

In terms of overall plot, the Gospel writers succeed splendidly in moving their stories progressively and inexorably toward a climactic conflict between Jesus and his enemies. In John's Gospel, we can trace, step by step, the development from the Jews' early debates with Jesus to a general plan to kill him. In the later phases of the story, the threat to Jesus is so dire that he travels secretly (11:54). As noted earlier, the same movement toward the climactic encounter can be seen in the references to the coming "hour" and to the actual arrival of the "hour." Following the triumphal entry, therefore, Jesus utters a discourse on the theme, "The hour has come for the Son of man to be glorified" (12:23–36).

As the story approaches the events of Christ's death, the focus constricts from Jesus' ministry in the world to his last days with his loyal disciples. The very details of the story reflect this constriction. Instead of miraculous signs that generate belief and unbelief in the crowds and religious leaders, Jesus now performs a sign for his disciples by washing their feet (13:1–20). The foot washing is another of Jesus' parabolic acts, combining action and meaning to teach spiritual truth in a manner similar to what we find in the miracles and parables of Jesus. The sin of unbelief, which had earlier involved large numbers of Jews, now becomes narrowed to unbelief within the disciples, as embodied in the dismissal of the traitor Judas Iscariot (13:21–30) and the prediction of Peter's denial (vv. 36–38). And in contrast to the earlier public discourses, Jesus now delivers a private address to the inner circle of disciples in the upper room (chaps. 14–16).

The discourse in the upper room belongs to the Hebraic literary form of the farewell address that an important person gives to his children or followers on the eve of his death.[12] Jesus' farewell address

12. The adherence of Jesus' discourse in the upper room to the Old Testament and intertestamental form of the farewell address is discussed by Raymond E. Brown, *The Gospel According to John, Thirteen to Twenty-one,* vol. 29A of the Anchor Bible (Garden City, N.Y.: Doubleday, 1970), pp. 597–601. Old Testament examples include the discourses of Jacob (Gen. 48–49), Moses (the Book of Deuteronomy), Joshua (Josh. 23–24), and David (1 Chron. 28–29). In the New Testament, 2 Peter shows some of the same motifs.

includes the following conventional motifs: the speaker's announcement of his imminent departure, the listeners' sorrow and accompanying words of comfort from the speaker, the directive to keep God's commandments, a command to the listeners to love one another, a prediction of what will happen to the listeners in the future, the invocation of peace upon the listeners, the naming of a successor (in this case, the Holy Spirit), and a concluding prayer for the listeners. The tone of Jesus' farewell address is intimate, loving, and full of compassionate concern for the disciples. In the background is the initiation motif, as the disciples are being introduced to the mission they will carry out in the absence of their master. The symbolic "I am" pronouncements that Jesus makes in John's Gospel here reach their culmination in the discourse about the true vine (15:1–6).

As is true of the other Gospels, the Gospel of John devotes a disproportionately large amount of space to the events surrounding the death of Jesus. In terms of narrative structure, the passion story in the Gospel of John unfolds in three stages—the betrayal (18:1–11), the trial (18:12–19:16), and the crucifixion (19:17–42). The betrayal is narrated summarily, while the trial is described in full circumstantial detail. The trial, in fact, is staged like a drama, and it is accordingly full of voices—voices questioning, accusing, denying, and demanding crucifixion.

One avenue to appreciating the storytelling technique of the passion stories is to note how skillful the writers were in selecting the significant detail in a style characterized by conciseness, economy, and understatement. A literary critic has described it thus:

> Mark tells of the crucifixion in twenty short verses, and even John does not go beyond thirty. Instead of attempting to portray what was impossible of description, they gave the effect upon the different observers— what the two robbers said, the mocking of the crowd, the testimony of the centurion, the weeping women, a convulsed earth and a black sky. This, with a few lines describing what was done, and a few words from the cross, paints the world's supreme tragedy. Note how noble is the restraint of the writers. There is no outburst of wrath against Judas, no condemnation of Herod, of Pilate, of the priests. The world's mightiest figure is set forth with no word of eulogy, with no attempt at heroics, no analysis of the feeling of the actors in events charged with emotion.[13]

The resurrection of Jesus from the grave (chap. 20) is the climax of John's Gospel, as it is of the others. It is the ultimate triumph of the

---

13. Charles Allen Dinsmore, *The English Bible as Literature* (Boston and New York: Houghton Mifflin, 1931), p. 265.

protagonist, proof of his uniqueness and divinity. It is also the ultimate example of the death-rebirth archetype. In terms of plot structure, the resurrection is the final phase of the U-shaped comic plot of the Gospel. The gradual isolation of the protagonist is now followed by his reintegration into society. It is evident that the inherent form of the New Testament Gospels is not tragedy but comedy.

The postresurrection appearances of Jesus are all structured as encounters with individuals. In terms of Gospel subtypes, they are recognition stories in which Jesus' followers come to recognize Jesus as their resurrected master. These are moments of high drama. Mary Magdalene's moment of surprised recognition is captured by her exclamation "Rabboni! [Master!]" (20:16). The story of the appearance to Thomas (20:24–29) is equally memorable, as Thomas's initial skepticism becomes muted in his exclamation of recognition and adoration, "My Lord and my God!" With this story, incidentally, the plot conflict between belief and unbelief that has unified John's Gospel reaches its final resolution.

The last event recorded in the story, the postresurrection appearance in which Jesus restores Peter (21:1–19), echoes key events in the Gospel and serves as a conclusion to the story that John has told. The mystery of Jesus' appearance at daybreak reminds us of a supernatural mystery that has pervaded the story from the prologue that gives a divine genealogy for the hero. The miraculous haul of fishes echoes an equally pervasive miraculous element in the story. The threefold restoration of Peter repeats the pattern of Peter's denial of Jesus and underscores the importance of patterns of repetition in John's Gospel.

John's Gospel in Retrospect

As we look back over the whole story that John has told, we might well ask what principle of organization accounts for the arrangement of the individual parts in their final form. If the Gospel writers were compilers of stories and sayings already in circulation, what pattern did they follow in weaving the individual units into the completed fabric? Although the general outline of events is chronological, the writers do not claim that each event is strictly chronological in its relation to other details. The Gospel of John, in particular, may deliberately dislocate chronology in order to achieve its ends. The arrangement of parts is not determined by theological considerations, since the theology would remain unchanged with other arrangements.

We can infer that the organization of John's Gospel is based on narrative principles. One of these is the principle of variety of episode. With a storyteller's instinct, John mingles long and short episodes, as well as mighty acts and spoken discourses. Events that carry their own meaning, such as the healing of the official's son, are interspersed with acts that are accompanied by interpretive discourses. Jesus' encounters with individuals are balanced by appearances to large crowds. Stories that end in belief are juxtaposed to episodes that lead to conflict and unbelief.

A second narrative principle that governs John's story is progression. We have observed the intensification of plot conflict as the story unfolds, the movement toward the climactic event of the execution of Jesus, and an expansion of Jesus' career from a private circle to the public arena, followed by a constriction to his disciples and friends.

Nor should we overlook the way in which John's Gospel is composed on the principles of unity, coherence, and emphasis. The unity consists of the presence of a central protagonist in every episode, as well as the existence of a plot conflict between Jesus and his opponents, and between belief and unbelief. The coherence of the story is enhanced by recurrent patterns, including the linking of a mighty sign by Jesus with a discourse that elaborates the same sign, the symbolic use of images such as bread and light to embody spiritual truth about Jesus, the motif of misunderstood sayings of Jesus, a series of "I am" pronouncements by Jesus, and number patterns. Out of these unifying elements emerges the emphasis on the worthiness and power of Jesus and the call to belief in him.

The Gospels as Stories

What is gained by reading the Gospels as complete and unified stories? To begin, such a reading is the only good corrective to the fragmentation that characterizes most people's experience of the Gospels. In most readers' minds, the Gospels are bewildering collections of fragments in which the individual units lack coherence with each other. How can this be right, when it is obvious that each Gospel writer took pains to arrange the individual units to best advantage and to cast them into a carefully designed narrative flow?

Once we accept the principle that a Gospel is a literary whole, we will find the total impact greatly enhanced. Individual units in the Gospel of John, for example, will have much more meaning for us if we can relate them to such overriding frameworks as the conflict between belief and unbelief, or the technique of matching Christ's great "signs" with discourses that expand them into symbols of spiritual realities, or the very human and moving story of Christ's worsening conflict with the Jewish authorities until they finally execute him.

It is an axiom of educational theory that isolated facts have little meaning until people can place them into a bigger unifying framework. The only adequate framework that I have found to unify the Gospels is to read them as continuous and whole stories. They are like modern serial stories in which the individual episodes are relatively self-contained but in which the units fit together in a movement toward a final goal.

Reading the Gospels as stories also gives us more accurate tools for analyzing them and talking about them. The Gospels are not a series of essays or sermons, though it is common to treat them as if they were. The Gospels are above all series of events performed by characters in specific settings. A basic principle of interpretation is that meaning is communicated *through* specific literary forms. Before we know what the Gospels teach, we need to ask the prior question of what happens to characters in a story.

Even the sayings and addresses embedded in the Gospels are placed in a narrative context. The famous sayings of Jesus are almost always linked with a specific narrative situation. The reason most people find it hard to think in terms of any larger literary unit than the individual proverb is that they have not been encouraged to think of the Gospels as whole stories.

Finally, the kind of narrative analysis I have urged opens the way for an artistic response to the Gospels. The Gospels are literary masterpieces that exhibit such artistic qualities as unity, coherence, and emphasis. They possess the adventure, excitement, and human interest of a novel or television drama. There is no reason to apologize for taking the time and effort to demonstrate that the Gospels are beautifully told stories that also contain beautiful poetry and proverbs. In fact, something is lacking if we do not find such beauty in them.

3

The Parables

The parables of Jesus are at once thoroughly literary and thoroughly laden with religious meaning. As for their literary dimension, they are the indisputable example of fiction in the Bible. They incarnate their meaning in story or metaphor in such a way that we cannot possibly ignore their literary nature. Yet they are a didactic genre that Jesus used to teach basic Christian doctrine and morality.

The parables also illustrate to perfection the double quality of much biblical literature. They require both a naive and a sophisticated response. On the surface they are the very touchstone of simplicity. They deal with the most realistic situations imaginable: a farmer sowing seed, a shepherd caring for sheep, a woman baking bread. But their complexity is such that scholars have produced an endless succession of books and articles on their meaning.

The parables exist on a continuum ranging from the simple to the complex. On the one end of the spectrum is the single metaphor or simile in which Jesus compares the kingdom of heaven to a mustard seed or lost coin or hidden treasure. At the other end is a relatively complex story with a skillfully designed plot, elaboration of setting and dialogue, and subtle characterization. In this chapter I will concentrate on the more complex parables that tell a story. To interpret the simple parables requires an ability to deal with metaphor and simile in the usual manner.

Literary Features of the Parables

Before explicating selected parables, I wish to note the literary features of the parables in general.[1] My excursions into the volumes of commentary that biblical scholars have produced on the parables in recent years have convinced me that the scholars have obscured the parables and isolated them from ordinary readers of the Bible. A genuinely literary approach can go a long way toward rehabilitating them for the people to whom Jesus gave them—ordinary people.

Folk Stories

The narrative appeal of the parables is the appeal of the folk story. These simple narratives exhibit virtually all of the features that have characterized popular storytelling through the ages.

One of these traits is the homespun realism that appeals to the most naive of literary tastes. The world of the parables is the world of the common people to whom Jesus preached—a world of fields, harvest, wedding invitations, household routine, or traveling to a neighboring town. The people who perform these actions are equally recognizable: they are farmers, migrant workers, fathers and sons, embezzlers, widows on a pension, merchants. Jesus has given us an unforgettable picture of peasant and bourgeois life in first-century Palestine. Corresponding to this thoroughgoing realism is the absence of fantasy elements such as talking animals or haunted forests.

The parables, in short, are based on the literary principle of verisimilitude (lifelikeness). They hold the mirror up to life. Reliance on precise, vivid illustrations is a standard technique in such literature, and here, too, the parables run true to form. "It is 'things' that make stories go well," writes a literary critic; in the parables everything "is concrete and vigorous ... [and] described in solid terms."[2] The Jesus of the parables reveals the gift of the master storyteller—"an amazing power of observation."[3]

1. For elaboration of the points I make in this section, see Leland Ryken, *How to Read the Bible as Literature* (Grand Rapids: Zondervan, 1984), pp. 139–53; and the excerpts from leading biblical scholars and literary critics in Leland Ryken, ed., *The New Testament in Literary Criticism*, A Library of Literary Criticism (New York: Ungar, 1984), pp. 255–72.

2. P. C. Sands, *Literary Genius of the New Testament* (New York: Oxford University Press, 1932), p. 86.

3. Geriant V. Jones, *The Art and Truth of the Parables* (London: S.P.C.K., 1964), p. 113. This is one of the best literary studies of the parables.

This power shows itself also at the level of characterization. Only one of the characters in the parables (Lazarus) is named. This anonymity helps to make the characters universal types. We know that we have met them, like the characters of Chaucer and Dickens, before. As Geriant V. Jones has aptly said, "Nowhere else in the world's literature has such immortality been conferred on anonymity" (p. 124).

The realism of the parables is an important part of their religious meaning. There are so few references to religious practices or to the religious professionals of the day that the surface world of the parables is decidedly "secular." On the basis of their literal level, we could not possibly guess that they are designed to teach religious truth. The parables thus assault any "two-world" outlook that divides the spiritual and earthly realms. In the world of the parables, it is in everyday experience that people make their spiritual decisions and that God's grace works.

The parables are oral folk stories, not only by virtue of the realism of their content, but also in their composition. They adhere to the rules or principles of folk stories through the centuries. Since I will apply these when I explicate selected parables, I will only list them here.

1. The rule of plot conflict.
2. The rule of suspense (generating curiosity about outcome).
3. The rule of contrast or foil.
4. The rule of simplicity or the single plot (absence of complicated situations or multiple actions). Part of the simplicity is the "dramatic rule of two," in which only two characters (or a character and a group) take part in the action at a given time (as in Greek drama).
5. The rule of repetition, especially threefold repetition.
6. The rule of end stress (the crucial element comes last, often as a foil to what has preceded).
7. The rule of universality, especially universal character types.

A final feature of the parables that links them to folk literature is their reliance on archetypes. Considered only as stories, the parables are too simple and brief to interest us. The presence of archetypes counteracts this effect. When Jesus tells stories about father and son, or about two sons, or about master (employer) and servant (employee), or about lost and found, our interest is assured.

Persuasion and Response

The parables are oral literature, which no doubt explains their brevity and simplicity. Their context in the Gospels makes it clear that

Jesus spoke the parables in the course of his teaching and debates with his opponents. In fact, some of the parables are Jesus' half of an argument.

Because of this context, the parables possess a strong persuasive element. They were addressed to specific audiences and designed to move listeners to a response. The parables are invitations and even traps designed to elicit a response. Knowing that listeners cannot absorb everything that they hear, Jesus told brief, memorable stories that do not carry all their meaning on the surface. They were intended to be carried away and pondered as a means of providing delayed-action insight (see Jesus' explanation of his method in Matthew 13: 10–17).

Satire and Subversion

There is a strong satiric element in the parables.[4] A number of them have a discernible object of attack. Sometimes the satire is the main point (e.g., the parables of the rich man and Lazarus and the Pharisee and the tax collector), while in others it is only one part of the overall design (as in the ecclesiastical satire against the priest and the Levite in the parable of the good Samaritan).

Even when the parables are not satiric, they tend to be subversive. This subversive quality stems particularly from the element of reversal of conventional values that underlies most of the parables. Regardless of what the specific theme of a parable is, there is often a deeper meaning as well. By introducing so many reversals of expectation, Jesus makes us question the reliability of our whole mindset.

For example, if Jesus wished simply to tell an example story about being compassionate to those in need, *any* character might have sufficed in the parable of the good Samaritan. But Jesus shocks us by making help come from the least likely source. Similarly, in the parable of the workers in the vineyard, the pay scale that takes no account of how long a person has worked runs counter to everything that we assume about fair employment practices. By means of these shocking reversals, Jesus conveys a sense of the completely new standards that prevail in the spiritual kingdom of God.

This element of reversal is signaled within the parables themselves by elements of unreality or exaggeration in predominantly realistic stories. Many of the parables contain a crack in the realism—some element that does not fit and that therefore teases us into seeing more

4. For more on satire in the parables, see chapter 14 of my companion volume to this book, *Words of Delight: A Literary Introduction to the Bible* (Grand Rapids: Baker, 1987).

in the parable than the literal level. Examples include a wedding feast for which all the invited guests find excuses not to come, an employer who pays the same wage regardless of how long his employees have worked, and a merchant who sells all his property to buy a single pearl.

Allegory in the Parables

Are the parables allegorical? Yes—they are. Despite all that some (though not all) biblical scholars have said to the contrary, the parables fit any standard literary definition of allegory. Elsewhere I have argued this in more detail,[5] and here I will simply discuss *how* the parables are allegorical.

The essential feature of allegory is that of double meaning: a detail in the story also stands for something else. If the term *allegory* has the wrong connotations because it smacks of the arbitrary and frivolous allegorizing that prevailed in the Middle Ages, we can use the synonym *symbol*. It is as simple as that.

There are several reasons why we cannot keep allegorical meanings out of the parables. Many of the images that Jesus used in the parables already had inherited symbolic meanings. Thus the owner of a vineyard is God, sowing seed is teaching or preaching the word of God, and a master who judges is God. Secondly, once we know that a parable is about a spiritual reality like the kingdom of God, the logic of the story itself demands that we interpret some of the details allegorically (symbolically). Most conclusive of all is the fact that Jesus himself interpreted two of his parables in an allegorical way (Matt. 13:18–23, 36–43).

Jesus' interpretation of these parables shows that he intended them as allegories. We should therefore note the crucial difference between *interpreting an allegorical text* and *allegorizing a text* that is not intended as allegory. When we ascribe corresponding other meanings to some of the details in a parable, we are interpreting a text that was intended to be allegorical.

A biblical scholar has devised a simple scheme for determining the allegorical content of the parables.[6] As he went through the parables, he listed the main details in each story and then counted how many of them have a corresponding other meaning. His conclusions: the allegorical content of the parables in the Gospel of Matthew is 82 percent, that in Mark 75 percent, and that in Luke 60 percent.

---

5. See Ryken, *How to Read the Bible as Literature*, pp. 145–51, 199–203.

6. M. D. Goulder, "Characteristics of the Parables in the Several Gospels," *Journal of Theological Studies* n.s. 19 (1968): 58–62.

The most helpful literary framework for discussing the allegory of the parables is Northrop Frye's idea of an allegorical continuum.[7] According to this scheme, *every* work of literature has an allegorical dimension to it. Furthermore, all commentary on the meaning of a literary work is allegorical in the sense that it translates the details of the story into a corresponding meaning. What we need, then, is not an approach that enables us to divide allegorical from nonallegorical works, but a framework that enables us to talk about the *degree* to which works of literature are allegorical.

This is where the concept of a sliding scale or continuum comes into play. At one end of the scale we find continuous allegory, in which virtually every detail has a corresponding meaning. In the middle we find incarnation, in which there is an obvious thematic intention but in which the ideas have been completely embodied in the story as a whole. At the far end of the spectrum we find realistic works with an abundance of surface detail with little obvious thematic intention. The allegorical continuum can be pictured as it is in figure 1.

The parables of Jesus range over the left half of this continuum. In the parable of the sower, for example, virtually every detail has a corresponding meaning. In the parable of the prodigal son, some of the details have an allegorical meaning (the father = God, the elder brother = the Pharisees), while others do not (the shoes and robe that the father gives to his son upon his return). In the middle of the spectrum we can place a parable like the story of the good Samaritan, in which the whole story embodies the meaning.

The basic principle of the parables is analogy or metaphor. A parable "elicits a judgment in one sphere in order to transfer it to another."[8] The metaphoric nature of the parables has sometimes been contrasted to allegory, but this is misleading. Allegory, too, is a bilevel

Figure 1 **The allegorical continuum**

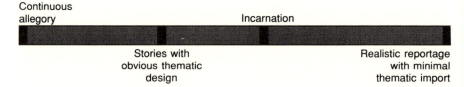

Continuous
allegory   Incarnation

Stories with   Realistic reportage
obvious thematic   with minimal
design   thematic import

7. Northrop Frye, *Anatomy of Criticism: Four Essays* (Princeton: Princeton University Press, 1957), pp. 89–92.

8. A. T. Cadoux, *The Parables of Jesus: Their Art and Use* (London: James Clarke, 1930), p. 56.

form. Indeed, as C. S. Lewis rightly points out, "every metaphor is an allegory in little."[9]

In both metaphor and allegory, one thing is compared to another. As Amos N. Wilder states, "there is the picture-side of the parable and there is the meaning or application."[10] The very word *parable* suggests allegory, since it literally means "to throw alongside." In the parables of Jesus, we do just that: we attach a corresponding meaning to some of the details in the story, either continuously or to the story as a whole. Allegorical reading of the parables actually enhances their metaphoric nature by introducing additional metaphors—God as father, for example, or the word of God as seed. Nonallegorical readings tend to reduce every parable to a single, very general meaning (recently the theme of reversal of values has been popular), and in the process they fail to do justice to the specificity of the text.

Explicating the Parables

The process of analyzing the parables and organizing a discussion of them falls naturally into the following four steps:

1. Narrative analysis (interacting with the story as a story).
2. Interpreting the allegory or symbolism of details that call for such interpretation.
3. Determining the theme(s) of the parable. This should not be confused with interpreting the allegory. In the parable of the talents, for example, to say that the owner of the talents is God and the return after a long journey is Christ's coming at the end of history is to interpret the allegory. To say that the parable teaches the need for good stewardship is to find the theme of the parable.
4. Application of the theme. Granted that a given theme is present, to whom does it apply, and how? There are two possible levels of application: how did it apply *then* (that is, in Jesus' day), and how does it apply *now?*

Knowing that I could explicate only a few of the parables, I have selected ones that illustrate something of the range of techniques that we find in the parables of Jesus.

9. C. S. Lewis, *The Allegory of Love: A Study in Medieval Tradition* (New York: Oxford University Press, 1936), p. 60.
10. Amos N. Wilder, *Early Christian Rhetoric: The Language of the Gospel* (Cambridge: Harvard University Press, 1971), p. 74.

The Parable of the Sower or Soils

The parable of the sower (Matt. 13:1–9, 18–23), more accurately called the parable of the soils, epitomizes the parable as a genre. The realism of the parable is fully evident. The kinds of soil that are the chief focus of the parable are exactly the ones that a farmer in Palestine would have encountered: the road that bordered the field and on which some seed invariably fell when the farmer broadcast it, the corners of a field where weeds dominate, the soil with an underlay of limestone, and the fertile soil. Nothing could have been more familiar to the experience of Jesus' original audience.

The story is too simple to interest us only on the surface level, yet it possesses enough narrative technique to make it effective for its didactic purpose. Three ingredients figure in the action—a sower, seed, and four kinds of soil. The types of soil are the variable in the story and are accordingly the key to its meaning. The main organizing principle is common in folk stories—threefold repetition. Further symmetry stems from the way in which the three unsatisfactory soils are balanced by three degrees of success in the fertile soil. An element of plot conflict is provided by the environment of struggle in which the seeds play out their destiny—an environment in which seeds are *devoured* and *choked* and *scorched*. The situation of entrusting seed to the earth also possesses the quality of an archetypal risk whose outcome is uncertain and therefore suspenseful.

Jesus himself provides an interpretation of the allegorical details in the parable (vv. 18–23). The seed is God's message of salvation and righteous living ("the word of the kingdom"). We infer (though this is the one detail in the story that Jesus does not allegorize) that the sower is the evangelist, or Jesus himself. The kinds of soil symbolize the responses of people who hear the word of God, which Jesus differentiates very specifically.

Several themes are embodied in this allegorical story. The preaching of the gospel is shown to occur in a context of spiritual warfare, with the result that it will inevitably meet with resistance. One cannot expect uniformly successful results from the preaching of the word. The parable shows, moreover, that salvation depends on the responses of people who hear the gospel (witness how the variable element is the soils). There is an assurance that the gospel will produce positive results in the lives of some listeners. Mainly, though, this is a parable about hearing. Its chief message is, *Take care how you listen and obey.*

What applications might this classification of responses by various types of listeners have had in Christ's day? Most interpreters of the parable believe that Jesus intended the parable as an encouragement to his disillusioned disciples. When the disciples saw the resistance that Jesus encountered, this theory states, they became discouraged and doubtful. Jesus told a parable that had the concept of fruitfulness and success as its climax in order to counteract their disillusionment.

I find this interpretation misleading. Matthew 13:2 makes it clear that Jesus was speaking to a large crowd of people, not simply to the disciples. The parable, moreover, concentrates on the kinds of soil, not the sower. The whole interest is focused on the soils, that is, the hearers of the gospel. This is a parable about how we listen, not about how we preach.

The parable was a challenge to those who were listening to the claims of the gospel to respond adequately to the message of the kingdom. Jesus delineates three inadequate responses to the message of the kingdom. The parable is thus a warning to the hearers of the gospel to avoid these errors. The harvest produced by the seed that fell in the fertile soil indicates an opportunity to choose a better way.

This application of the parable is timeless. The options are the same today as they were in Jesus' day. The choices with which Jesus confronted his first listeners are the same ones that he puts before people today.

The Parable of the Generous Employer

The parable of the sower belongs to the category of parables of action, inasmuch as the point of the parable turns on what happens to the seed that is sown, not on the character of the sower. But other parables hinge on the dynamics of human character. The parable of the workers in the vineyard and their generous employer (Matt. 20: 1–16) typifies the parables of character.

The plot is simply a framework on which Jesus hangs his character study. It is based on the principle of fivefold repetition, as the owner of the vineyard, harried by the pressure of harvest, goes to the marketplace at five different times of the day to enlist workers for his vineyard. The motif on which the plot is based is simply labor and its reward. Hiring the workers in the first part of the parable is balanced by payment at the end.

The pressure point of the parable comes at the end and centers on the character of the employer. He pays everyone the same wage, regardless of how long people had worked. This is equivalent to giving every student the same grade in a course, with no questions asked. Given conventional standards of fair play, the employees who had worked longest naturally complained. The insight into human psychology is thoroughly realistic at this point.

But more important is the question of what kind of person the employer is. Is he just? If not, what is he? He is just because he has fulfilled the conditions of his contract with the workers: *Did you not agree with me for a denarius?* (v. 13). But the parable is not primarily about justice: it is about generosity, as the employer's parting shot in the parable suggests: *Or do you begrudge my generosity?* (v. 15). A denarius was a living wage, and the fact that the employer was concerned that everyone, even those who worked only one hour, would receive a denarius proves his compassion. Within the logic of the parable, the owner of the vineyard emerges as a generous man, with the grumbling workers functioning as a foil that heightens his generosity. (Conversely, the generosity and compassion of the employer point out the moral failure of the workers who complain.)

As a literary form, the parable "elicits a judgment in one sphere in order to transfer it to another" (Cadoux, p. 56). This parable is a good example. We are intended to transfer what the parable demonstrates about the owner of the vineyard to God. In fact, several details in the parable must be interpreted allegorically. The owner of the vineyard is God, the workers in the vineyard are believers, working in the vineyard is doing God's work in the world, the payment is salvation, and the equality of payment means that all believers will be glorified in heaven. The theme hinges particularly on this last item: salvation depends on the generosity of God, not on human merit.

Viewed thus, the parable illustrates the subversive reversal of conventional values that pervades the parables. Who ever heard of a pay scale that pays no attention to how long the workers have been on the job? The aphorism with which Jesus concludes the parable focuses exactly on this rejection of conventional human standards: *So the last will be first, and the first last* (v. 16). That is, in the kingdom of God where generosity is the foundational premise, ordinary human standards have been abolished.

The application to Jesus' original audience is fairly obvious. Jesus here anticipates what would become one of the great issues in the early church: the Gentiles could be saved without the encumbrances of the ceremonial laws that the Jews had performed for centuries. Was this fair? The parable at least provides a perspective from which an answer might emerge.

But the application of the parable is more extensive than that. In any religious group, the disparity of commitment and spiritual exertion among members is immense. Do the slackers deserve salvation? Here, too, the parable of the generous employer, with its implicit rejection of human merit as a criterion for salvation, provides an answer.

The Parable of the Good Samaritan

The parable of the good Samaritan (Luke 10:25–37) provides a contrast to the previous parables. In it, Jesus avoids continuous allegory and instead tells an example story that falls in the middle of the allegorical continuum. The whole story is the meaning, and we do not translate individual details into a corresponding meaning. We simply observe examples of virtue to follow and vice to avoid. The theme of the parable, moreover, is not (as in most of the parables) theological but ethical.

Jesus tells the parable as part of a debate with an opponent, as the introduction makes clear with its explanation that *a lawyer stood up to put him to the test* (v. 25). It is important to our understanding of the parable to realize, therefore, that this story is Jesus' answer to the lawyer's question, *And who is my neighbor?* (v. 29). Jesus does, however, subtly shift the focus from defining who the lawyer's neighbor is to the more personal question of how to *be* a neighbor.

The story as a whole epitomizes the folk qualities of the parables. The main narrative premise is the *test* motif, as the wounded man on the road becomes a test of the compassion of three passersby. The story opens with some violent *plot conflict* to grab our attention: "he fell among robbers, who stripped him and beat him, and departed, leaving him half dead" (v. 30). The plot pattern of *threefold repetition* also provides structure, as we see a common event (a passerby observes the wounded man) three times, with a crucial change introduced the third time. The technique of *foil* is therefore also important to the dynamics of the story, as we observe a heightened contrast between virtue and vice.

The parable begins with precise realism. The violence that occurred on the road between Jerusalem and Jericho was notorious. We read that the lone traveler *was going down from Jerusalem to Jericho* (v. 30). The trip does, in fact, involve a drastic descent in altitude. Similar realism underlies the account of a priest going down the same route as the victim had taken. In Christ's day many priests who served in Jerusalem actually lived in Jericho. We are not told why the priest passed by on the other side. He may have simply lacked compassion. In the background lies the practice of robbers who used supposedly wounded people as decoys, putting travelers at a disadvantage if they stooped over the decoy to investigate. Whatever the reason for the priest's action, he introduces the element of satire into the parable, as Jesus exposes the moral failure of a religious leader.

The Levite who passes by reinforces the ecclesiastical satire against the religious elite of Jesus' day. Levites were also ministers in the temple. There was a Jewish ceremonial law (Num. 19:11) that made anyone who touched a dead body unclean for seven days. If the Levite was en route to a stint of service in Jerusalem, he may have been deterred from helping the wounded man by the fact that he would have been unable to carry out his religious function for a whole week. If this is the drift of the parable, we can begin to see its complexity, despite its surface simplicity: established religious rules are in conflict with moral compassion for people in need.

The pattern of threefold repetition reaches its climax with the behavior of the Samaritan, and here, too, we see the subversive assault on the deep structure of conventional thinking. Jesus makes compassion come from the least likely (and most despised) source. The unexpectedness of the situation is heightened by the fact that the Jews of Jesus' day thought in terms of the triad priest-Levite-Israelite. Here the third person is a Samaritan, a race so hated that when the lawyer is asked to identify the neighbor in the parable, he cannot bring himself to name the Samaritan and instead replies, *the one who showed mercy on him* (v. 37).

To accentuate the basic shock of the situation, Jesus uses the rule of proportionate space to focus our attention on the virtuous behavior of the unlikely benefactor. A biblical scholar notes that

> in Greek, there are forty-six words given to what precedes the arrival of the Samaritan on the scene but sixty words devoted to his arrival and, step-by-step, to his reaction. Since this reaction is so unexpected, it must be spelled out in explicit detail. The hearer must not be able to shrug it off by saying: No Samaritan would act that way! He must feel instead: I have just seen the wine and the oil, the donkey, and the inn. I have just seen the two denarii exchange hands.[11]

This is obviously a parable of action. It was occasioned by the lawyer's question, "What shall I *do* to inherit eternal life?" (v. 25). Jesus' final words underscore that the parable has, indeed, been a parable of doing: "Go and *do* likewise" (v. 37).

As this parting statement suggests, the parable of the good Samaritan is an example story that pictures a model of virtue to emulate. There is no better illustration of how the dominant aim of Jesus' parables is the persuasive one of moving the listener to a response. The parable itself is Jesus' literary definition of *neighbor* and as such shows how the imagination embodies truth instead of telling us about

11. John Dominic Crossan, *The Dark Interval: Towards a Theology of Story* (Niles, Ill.: Argus, 1975), pp. 107–8.

it abstractly. We do not have to turn this parable into a proposition in order to assimilate its truth. All we need to do is recognize the neighborly behavior of the Samaritan and the moral deficiency of the priest and the Levite.

The Parable of the Prodigal Son and the Forgiving Father

The most literary of Jesus' parables is the one commonly known as the parable of the prodigal son but perhaps better called the parable of the forgiving father (Luke 15:11–32).[12] Here we have a fully developed story with complication of action and subtlety of characterization. The three-phase story concentrates on the relationships among the three main characters.

Like many of Jesus'· parables, this one is his half of an argument. The context of the parable is that "the Pharisees and the scribes murmured, saying, 'This man receives sinners and eats with them' " (v. 2). In replying, Jesus told two short parables (the parables of the lost sheep and lost coin) that stress God's joy in receiving repentant sinners into fellowship. The story of the lost son, the forgiving father, and the older brother who refuses reconciliation is the climax of this triad of parables on a common theme.

This is the most archetypal of Jesus' parables. The journey of withdrawal and return is common among the stories of the world. It is a death-rebirth story and a story of initiation (into sin and its consequences). The prodigal is an archetypal character who represents an impulse that lies within each of us. It is the impulse away from the domestic, the secure, and the governed, toward the distant, the adventurous, the rebellious, the indulgence of forbidden appetites (including the sexual), the abandonment to unrestraint. The older brother of the parable represents an equally recognizable part of our psychological make-up: the voice of duty, restraint, self-control, and self-righteousness, cold and rigid when it encounters its opposite. It is no wonder that one of these is the *younger* son (a figure of youth with its thirst for experience and abandonment to appetite) and the other the *older* son (with its middle-aged mentality).

Also important to our response to the literal level of the parable is the fact that it is a family situation. There are feelings of parent toward child, for example, that cannot be put into words but that are accurately portrayed in the picture of the father's relationship to both of his sons. We also know experientially what happens at the end of the parable. It is called sibling rivalry and here takes the form of hurt

12. For some superb commentary and appreciative statements on this parable, I recommend the excerpts in *The New Testament in Literary Criticism*, pp. 285–94.

from a feeling that a parent has unfairly favored one's sibling. In short, almost everything that happens in the parable taps deep springs of archetypal feeling.

The realistic description and dialogue in the parable enhance its archetypal richness. Everything is concrete and tangible. We picture poverty as hunger for hog feed, forgiveness as a father embracing a son and putting a robe, ring, and shoes on him, and jealousy as the charge that the father never gave the older son *a kid, that [he] might make merry with [his] friends*. Here emotions are translated at once into action and image. The movement of the plot is quick and decisive, as are the speeches of the characters.

There are many famous first sentences in the stories of the world, but none more famous than this one: *There was a man who had two sons . . .* (v. 11). It is one of the memorable moments of literature. The opening action is equally memorable: the younger son arrogantly asks for his share of the inheritance, which in its cultural setting was equivalent to saying that he wished that his father were dead. Once we have assimilated this opening shock, we encounter another: the father takes it all in stride and gives his son the money he has requested.

The son's *journey into a far country* (v. 13) is archetypal. It is a primordial image of human experience whose application is never exhausted. We are all "lost children." The spectacle of immoral indulgence of appetites is told with stark simplicity: *he squandered his property in loose living* (v. 13). At this point the son's fortunes take a turn that we could predict, given the archetypal pattern at work here: *and when he had spent eveything, a great famine arose in that country, and he began to be in want* (v. 14).

As in the story of the fall itself, loss leads to initiation, here an initiation into the adult world of labor and deprivation. A few details portray the depths into which the son falls as a consequence of his sin and folly: *So he went and joined himself to one of the citizens of that country, who sent him into his fields to feed swine. And he would gladly have fed on the pods that the swine ate; and no one gave him anything* (vv. 15–16). Not only were hogs unclean animals for the Jews: to eat the food of hogs would reduce the prodigal to a subhuman level, yet even this is denied him. No wonder the father will twice describe his son as having been *dead*. Here is the essence of human tragedy.

Equally true to the pattern of literary tragedy is the way in which the son's suffering leads to his moral and intellectual growth. The turning point in his development comes when he reaches a perception of his moral failing. The parable puts it in unforgettable terms: *he came to himself* (v. 17) and was ready to admit to his father, *Father, I have sinned against heaven and before you; I am no longer worthy to be called your son* (vv. 18–19). This awareness of bankruptcy is combined with a resolve to return to his father: *he said, "How many of my father's hired servants have bread enough and to spare, but I perish here with hunger! I will arise and go to my father"* (vv. 17–18). Here is the moment of recognition that is common to narrative in general and tragedy in particular.

The surface realism of this parable is as striking as the spiritual realities that it embodies. The son's comment about his father's *hired servants* must be understood in terms of the three kinds of employees in the Jewish culture of the day. The categories were bondmen (slaves with good family standing), servants (subordinates of the slaves), and hired servants (hired for the occasion). The son who reached for everything has bottomed out on the social scale of his society.

As impressive as the realism of the opening phase of the story is, we are aware as we read it of the enormous human realities being portrayed by it. We have here an analysis of freedom abused, moral degeneracy, human accountability, estrangement, loss, anguish, longing, self-laceration over one's failure, physical suffering, and (at the end) the courage to confess and repent. Where have so few sentences ever captured so much of the human condition?

In the second phase of the action, the character and actions of the father become the focus of interest. The father reverses our expectations of disapproval by showing forgiveness and exuberant compassion toward his wayward son before the latter has even had a chance to confess. Following the formal confession speech (which we hear for the second time in the parable in verse 21), the father rejects the son's offer to be accepted as a hired servant and instead commands, *Bring quickly the best robe, and put it on him; and put a ring on his hand, and shoes on his feet; and bring the fatted calf and kill it, and let us eat and make merry* (vv. 22–23).

All of these details convey deeper meanings rooted in the cultural context assumed in the parable. The robe symbolizes (in a sense distinct from allegory) the honor with which the son is received into family fellowship. The ring, a signet ring, signifies the exalted status of the son, who is granted the rights and authority of the ruling family instead of being subordinated as a slave. The shoes also represent his status as a son, since slaves went barefoot. And as for the fatted calf that is slain, it is an evocative biblical archetype, with connotations of honor, hospitality, and extravagant celebration.

In the third act of this drama, Jesus turns the parable into a satiric attack on the scribes and the Pharisees. The occasion for the parable, we should remember, was the Pharisees' complaint that Jesus associated with sinners. This is exactly the attitude that is embodied in the elder brother. As a literary character, he belongs to a familiar archetype from literature, the unsympathetic refuser of festivities. The father tries to mediate between his two sons, but the elder brother remains incorrigibly self-centered and unforgiving, isolated from the drama of forgiveness in which he is invited to participate. Each of the sons thus misbehaves in his own way, while the father emerges as the generous and forgiving central figure in the picture.

The parable communicates rich meanings simply at a human level. But that is not its only purpose. Jesus told this parable in a specific context that helps us to interpret the allegory. The persuasive purpose of the parable as a reply to Jesus' accusers emerges only if we make the equations of the father as God, the prodigal as human sinner, the older brother as scribe and Pharisee, the son's return as an illustration of repentance, and the father's acceptance of his son as God's forgiveness of sinners. Furthermore, the language of the father's speech explaining his joy (a speech that we hear twice) is unmistakably theological: *for this my son was dead, and is alive again; he was lost, and is found* (v. 24; see also v. 32).

By interacting with the story at its narrative and allegorical levels, we have already observed its themes. This parable is a marvelously compressed picture of such universal psychological and spiritual realities as sin, guilt, repentance, and forgiveness. And the application is universal and timeless.

The parable of the prodigal son epitomizes Jesus' parables. It exhibits the narrative qualities of the parable as a literary form—the realism, the folk conventions, the archetypal richness, the sheer humanity, the allegorical or symbolic overtones of many of the details in the story. Here we find literary artistry, profundity combined with simplicity, elemental emotion, and spiritual intensity.

4

The Book of Acts

It is an easy step from the Gospels to the Book of Acts. Both are collections of relatively self-contained stories with interspersed speeches. A loose chronological principle organizes the individual units. We also find the familiar mingling of three dominant impulses—the didactic impulse to teach religious truth, the documentary impulse to record historical information about events, and the literary impulse to recreate experiences in vivid and concrete detail.

The Book of Acts provides a good test case for the underlying thesis of this book—that the New Testament literary forms are not totally new but represent a modification of traditional literary types. The Book of Acts is much closer to our familiar literary experiences than we have been led to think.

Unique Features of the Book of Acts

The title of the book—*The Acts of the Apostles*—itself suggests something of the novelty of what we find here. As the title suggests, the book lacks a single protagonist. But of course so do many of the Old Testament narrative books. If we streamline slightly, we might say that Peter dominates the first half of the book and Paul the second half. Or perhaps we might view either the church or the Holy Spirit as the central character who is present from beginning to end. In any case, the multiplicity of focus makes this story unusual. We are reminded of the genre of biography at many points in the book, though the book as a whole is not biographical.

The content of the book, secondly, makes it different from the stories that we read elsewhere. It is filled with unique, once-only events, unlike the more universal or representative occurrences that most stories present. The history of the early church by eyewitnesses is a unique subject for a story. The writer keeps the focus very steadily on this subject, so that the events we encounter strike us as unusual material for a story.

The Book of Acts as Story

The things that make the book unique are minor compared with the familiar literary features of the book. In such areas as unified structure, narrative techniques, dramatic scenes and speeches, and unifying images, the Book of Acts emerges as a thoroughly recognizable literary phenomenon.[1]

Structure and Unity

The structure of the book can be plotted in several ways, depending on how simple or detailed we wish the arrangement to be. The simplest scheme is twofold. In the first half of the book, the church discovers its identity. In the second half, it reaches out into the world. The latter story is synonymous with the missionary journeys of Paul.

A threefold outline sees the book as falling into the following units: events in Jerusalem (1–5), the church's mission in Palestine and Syria (6–12), and the mission and imprisonment of Paul (13–28). There is a gradual constriction from a crowded background of characters and events to the journeys of a single person.

Even more customary is the sixfold arrangement of the book: the founding of the church in Jerusalem (1:1–6:7); the dispersal of Christians throughout Palestine after the martyrdom of Stephen (6:8–9:31); the spread of the church to Syria (9:32–12:25); Paul's first missionary journey, to Asia Minor (13:1–16:5); Paul's journeys to Macedonia and Greece (16:6–21:14); Paul's carrying of the gospel to Rome as a prisoner (21:15–28:31). Seen thus, the organizing principle of the story is

1. For a wealth of literary commentary on the Book of Acts, see the collected excerpts in Leland Ryken, ed., *The New Testament in Literary Criticism*, A Library of Literary Criticism (New York: Ungar, 1984), pp. 42–61. My commentary in this chapter is indebted at every turn to these sources.

a succession of waves by which the Christian gospel advances from Jerusalem to Rome.

The journey and quest motifs are obviously important in the patterns I have noted. The outward expansion of the church is not a random wandering but a purposeful quest to conquer the world with the Christian gospel. There is a strong sense of movement toward a goal. Of course, there is a surprise at the very end of the book. The story ends abruptly, with Paul's mission to Rome left incomplete. This open-ended conclusion is an impressive version of the technique of the serial story, with its premise "to be continued." The story told in the Book of Acts did not end but is still continuing.

All this emphasis on travel and geography helps to supply some of the master images that unify the story. Chief among these are the journey and the city. The journeys of the apostles and missionaries assume the symbolic force of "the Way" (see 9:2; 16:17; 18:26; 19:9, 23; 24:14, 22). The journey of Paul as a prisoner bound for Rome has the overtones of a Via Dolorosa (the way of sorrow; that is, the way of the cross), a journey of suffering for Christ. The image of the city also recurs in the story and is one of the things that gives the Book of Acts its modern flavor.

Along with the progressive element in the story, the book is structured on a cyclic principle. The following pattern is repeated throughout the book in an ever-widening spiral: Christian leaders arise and preach the gospel; God performs mighty acts through them; listeners are converted and added to the church; opponents (usually Jewish) begin to persecute the Christian leaders; God intervenes to rescue the leaders or otherwise protect the church.[2]

Geography is a major organizing principle in the Book of Acts. I have already noted that the progression of the plot involves geographic expansion outward from Jerusalem. The story begins in Jerusalem and ends in Rome, and there is a symbolic importance in this strategy. Jerusalem represents the Jewish roots from which Christianity arose. Rome is the capital of the Gentile world. The geographical transfer that occurs in the Book of Acts is also a theological transfer.

The foregoing discussion of the structure of the book suggests why some commentators have ascribed an epic quality to Acts. The story has epic sweep. It is the story not of an individual but of a whole group. The epic sense of destiny breathes through the book. Equally epic is the expansion of the action over vast stretches of geography.

---

2. M. D. Goulder's *Type and History in Acts* (London: S.P.C.K., 1964) is a book-length treatment of Acts in terms of this cyclic structure.

Storytelling Technique

The Book of Acts is not an ecclesiastical history filled with names and dates. It is a story. Its preoccupation is not with institutions and church organization but with personalities and events. The story of Acts is built around a gallery of character portraits and a series of memorable events. In this story we meet such varied characters as kings and rulers, rabbis and high priests, ordinary people like Simon the tanner and Lydia the seller of cloth, and the intellectual elite of the Greeks known as the Areopagus.

The story, moreover, is an adventure story. The Book of Acts gives us twenty-eight chapters packed with trials, riots, persecutions, escapes, martyrdoms, voyages, shipwrecks, and rescues. And all of this action takes place in the major cities of the ancient world—Jerusalem, Antioch, Philippi, Corinth, Athens, Ephesus, and Rome. There is an equal variety in the settings: temples, prisons, courts, deserts, ships, seas, barracks, and theaters. To catch the full effect of this adventure, we need to read the whole book in one or two sittings.

As an adventure story, the Book of Acts makes use of a narrative pattern that is familiar in stories wherever they are told—the narrow escape. "Paul's story," writes William A. Beardslee, "is made up of a whole series of narrow escapes," with "further depth . . . given to the narrow escape theme by the fact that Paul's career is paralleled on a smaller scale by the narrow escapes of Peter."[3]

Storytellers select their material carefully, often with a view toward making the few details that they include add up to a total picture. There can be little doubt that the writer of Acts chose events that are *representative*. Examples include preaching in the temple (3), the apostles before the Sanhedrin (4:13–22; 5:17–32), the working of signs (3), the election and ordination of church officers (6:1–6), and a martyrdom (7).

Similarly, we attend a sabbath service in a synagogue (13:13–52), a church assembly to settle an issue of church policy (15:1–21), and a Christian worship service (20:7–12). We listen to a typical sermon to Jews (2:14–42), a typical address to Greek philosophers (17), a typical appeal to pagans ignorant of the Christian message (14:8–18), and a typical defense before a Roman govenor (24). We also witness a riot in Ephesus (19:23–41). Storytellers cannot include everything that happened, but they can select the significant particular that suggests the bigger picture.

3. William A. Beardslee, *Literary Criticism of the New Testament*, Guides to Biblical Scholarship: New Testament series, ed. Dan Otto Via, Jr. (Philadelphia: Fortress, 1970), p. 51.

Despite the uniqueness of its events, the story of Acts is built around universal or archetypal patterns. Archetypal motifs include imprisonment, attack, rescue, journey, quest, trial, sea voyage, and the city. Recent literary commentary on Acts has uncovered a host of parallels in the literature of ancient Greece and Rome.

The Book of Acts is famous for its drama. Its dramatic flavor is evident in the prevalence of oral forms (dialogue, address, sermon, courtroom defense), emphasis on the settings in which events occur, and attention to the dramatic gestures of characters. In the Book of Acts, we find an abundance of all these. In fact, dramatized speeches in their settings account for nearly 75 percent of the book. The setting for Paul's defense before Agrippa is typical of the dramatic flavor of the book as a whole:

> So on the morrow Agrippa and Bernice came with great pomp, and they entered the audience hall with the military tribunes and the prominent men of the city. Then by command of Festus Paul was brought in. . . .
> Agrippa said to Paul, "You have permission to speak for yourself."
> Then Paul stretched out his hand and made his defense:
> "I think myself fortunate that it is before you, King Agrippa, I am to make my defense today against all the accusations of the Jews. . . ."
> [25:23; 26:1–2]

"The story of Paul before Agrippa," writes P. C. Sands in his invaluable book on the literary aspects of the New Testament, "is as stirring as that of Elijah on Mount Carmel."[4]

A final thing to note about the storytelling technique of Acts is the realism with which the story is told. Sands catches the essence of the style with these examples:

> Converts in Athens *'glued themselves'* to Paul . . . , and Paul and his company *'tear themselves away'* from the elders of Ephesus. . . . Apollos was *'boiling'* in spirit or *'fervent'*, the audience at Pentecost were *'pricked* in their heart', and Stephen's hearers were *'cut to the heart'* (lit. sawn asunder), Paul *'makes havoc of'* (lit. 'sacks') those who believed (pp. 121–22).

The Book of Acts combines the familiar and the unfamiliar. Its subject matter is unique, and as a story it is more miscellaneous than we ordinarily expect a story to be. But in terms of narrative structure and storytelling technique, it is a thoroughly recognizable literary work.

---

4. P. C. Sands, *Literary Genius of the New Testament* (New York: Oxford University Press, 1932), p. 116.

Luke's narrative and dramatic abilities so impressed Ernest Renan that he spoke of "a new Homer."

The Story of Peter's Rescue

To illustrate the narrative and artistic qualities of Acts, I have chosen to explicate the story of Peter's rescue from prison as told in chapter 12. The reading that I give to this specimen will illustrate the kind of richness that other parts of the book also possess.

The appeal of the story derives partly from the story pattern itself, the rescue motif. This archetype provides the structure for the story, which can be organized around the threefold pattern of the antecedents, occurrence, and aftermath of the rescue. The opening paragraph of the story establishes the situation that makes the rescue possible:

> ¹About that time Herod the king laid violent hands upon some who belonged to the church. ²He killed James the brother of John with the sword; ³and when he saw that it pleased the Jews, he proceeded to arrest Peter also. This was during the days of Unleavened Bread. ⁴And when he had seized him, he put him in prison, and delivered him to four squads of soldiers to guard him, intending after the Passover to bring him out to the people. ⁵So Peter was kept in prison; but earnest prayer for him was made to God by the church.

Here is the first necessary ingredient of a rescue story—the danger or threat that renders the hero of the story helpless. To heighten the danger, this story locates the threat in a villain, the archetypal evil king with absolute power to annihilate people whom he dislikes.

Almost every detail in the first four verses adds to the threat and the seeming helplessness of the situation. In the New Testament, the very name *Herod* is synonymous with terror, with the epithet *Herod the king* adding the connotations of anti-Christian tyranny. To say that this king *laid violent hands upon* Christians is to give us a physical sense of the terror. The mention in the opening verse of the antagonism between Herod and *the church* introduces the plot conflict between other religions and Christianity, between the power structure of the state and a small, persecuted religious minority.

In verse 2, the account of the murder of James is callously brief, suggesting something of the swiftness of the murder itself. The execution is made vivid to our imaginations when we are told that James was killed *with the sword*. Verse 3 enlarges on this hostility against the Christians by indicating the Jews' approval of Herod's crime. All the Jewish hostility delineated in the Gospels and the Book of Acts here becomes aimed against Peter, the leader of the Christian church in Jerusalem. Herod is suddenly the most dangerous type of villainous king—the one who hopes to win favor with his constituency by killing leaders of a religious minority.

Verse 4 adds to the spectacle by locating us within the echoing walls of a prison, with the hopelessness of Peter's situation intensified by the enormous safeguard of *four squads of soldiers to guard him*. There may be a hint of foreshadowing here, making us wonder if Herod suspected that something might thwart his plans to kill Peter when the Passover was finished. The further reference to Herod's waiting until the Passover was over *to bring him out to the people* draws the terror to a crescendo, with the dread reinforced by our awareness that this desire to avoid bloodshed on the Passover was what happened at the execution of Jesus.

The first four verses of the story have been an ever-expanding vision of terror and helplessness. Verse 5 has a sudden calming effect. Counteracting all the terror are such spiritual resources as prayer, a caring group of Christians, and God in heaven. The evocative last clause introduces a solemn note of hope into the vision of terror: *but earnest prayer for him was made to God by the church.*

From the general situation we move to the critical last night of the Passover, the night before the planned execution. In verse 6 the writer renders the helpless plight of Peter in full visual detail:

> The very night when Herod was about to bring him out, Peter was sleeping between two soldiers, bound with two chains, and sentries before the door were guarding the prison.

It is no wonder that painters have seen the visual potential of the moment. Escaping is obviously the last thing that Peter expected. We notice also the inspiring picture of the hero peaceful in the face of death.

Verse 7 introduces the third essential ingredient in a rescue story, in addition to the threat and the helpless victim, namely, the agent of rescue. In this story, it is an angel, resplendent in supernatural light:

> And behold, an angel of the Lord appeared, and a light shone in the cell; and he struck Peter on the side and woke him, saying, "Get up quickly." And the chains fell off his hands.

The shining divine light is one of the great archetypes of the Bible. Here that supernatural aura is mingled with something as mundane as striking a sleeping person to awaken him.

The description of the rescue continues in the next two verses:

⁸And the angel said to him, "Dress yourself and put on your sandals." And he did so. And he said to him, "Wrap your mantle around you and follow me." ⁹And he went out and followed him; he did not know that what was done by the angel was real, but thought he was seeing a vision.

The very details that the storyteller gives us here convey how the benumbed Peter moves as if in a dream. Peter is childlike in the scene. With just a few details the writer makes the event come alive.

In verse 10 the supernatural or miraculous merges with the everyday physical world:

When they had passed the first and the second guard, they came to the iron gate leading into the city. It opened to them of its own accord, and they went out and passed on through one street; and immediately the angel left him.

We have all stood in an empty city street in the darkness and know something of the feelings of fear, vulnerability, loneliness, and exposure that drive one to seek refuge. This is the situation of Peter in his state of semiconsciousness.

Only in verse 11 does the recipient of this miraculous rescue come to full consciousness:

And Peter came to himself, and said, "Now I am sure that the Lord has sent his angel and rescued me from the hand of Herod and from all that the Jewish people were expecting."

It has taken Peter about as long to gain awareness as it does a teenager at the breakfast table. Here is his moment of epiphany (insight) into the meaning of the event. The very brevity of the account of the rescue, with everything concentrated in a few vivid details, takes us through the swift excitement of the event itself.

The story of what happens next is likewise so famous that it is impossible to retell the story of the rescue without this sequel. It is the story of the interrupted prayer meeting:

¹²When he realized this, he went to the house of Mary, the mother of John whose other name was Mark, where many were gathered together and were praying. ¹³And when he knocked at the door of the gateway, a maid named Rhoda came to answer. ¹⁴Recognizing Peter's voice, in her joy she did not open the gate but ran in and told that Peter was standing at the gate. ¹⁵They said to her, "You are mad." But she insisted

that it was so. They said, "It is his angel!" [16]But Peter continued knocking; and when they opened, they saw him and were amazed. [17]But motioning to them with his hand to be silent, he described to them how the Lord had brought him out of the prison. And he said, "Tell this to James and to the brethren." Then he departed and went to another place.

What we have here is a delightful foil (contrast and echo) to the story of the rescue. After the terror of the prison, we have the safe and homey associations of the house of Mary. Instead of the sinister gates and soldiers of the prison, we have a maid named Rhoda answering the door of the gateway. (A student, incidentally, identified Rhoda as the archetypal airhead, though other characters in the episode qualify for the same title.)

After all the tension of what happens in the prison during the rescue, we have the undercurrent of humor in this episode, climaxing in the absurd suggestion that it is Peter's angel knocking at the door. After the swift, purposeful actions of the rescue, we now witness confusion of action at the prayer meeting. The opened gates of the prison contrast with the gate that remains closed to Peter here, as Peter finds it easier to get out of prison than into a prayer meeting. The angel had led Peter out of prison; here the hapless Peter is momentarily identified as his own angel. In the first story, Peter was amazed; here the people around him are said to be amazed.

Putting these two episodes beside each other, we find the epitome of two tendencies that recur throughout the Bible. On the one hand we encounter miraculous, more-than-earthly activity. On the other, we recognize actions so familiar to our own experience that they could have happened in our own family or neighborhood or church during a typical week. The Bible as a whole is filled with both types of material.

At first sight we might think that the story of Peter's rescue is complete with his exit from the scene. But it is a narrative principle that an action is complete only when the issues that have been introduced are resolved. The story opened not with Peter, but with the wicked Herod and his elaborate intentions to persecute the church. At the end of the story, therefore, we return to Herod. The first piece of narrative business is to show us the aftermath of the rescue back at the prison the next morning:

[18]Now when day came, there was no small stir among the soldiers over what had become of Peter. [19]And when Herod had sought for him and could not find him, he examined the sentries and ordered that they should be put to death. Then he went down from Judea to Caesarea, and remained there.

As readers, we are naturally curious to know the repercussions of the miraculous rescue in the camp of the enemy. In keeping with the logic of a miracle story, this scene helps to authenticate the miracle. We note, too, another element in the coherence of the story: Peter's appearance had caused commotion at Mary's house, and now his disappearance causes commotion at the prison and court.

Balancing the opening reference to Herod's grand and evil schemes against the church, the story ends with an account of Herod's untimely death:

> [20]Now Herod was angry with the people of Tyre and Sidon; and they came to him in a body, and having persuaded Blastus, the king's chamberlain, they asked for peace, because their country depended on the king's country for food. [21]On an appointed day Herod put on his royal robes, took his seat upon the throne, and made an oration to them. [22]And the people shouted, "The voice of a god, and not of man!" [23]Immediately an angel of the Lord smote him, because he did not give God the glory; and he was eaten by worms and died.

There is a good narrative rationale for the inclusion of this material. The chapter began with Herod's wicked experiment in living, which consisted of an attempt to exalt himself by killing Christian leaders. In order for this story to be complete, we need to see the outcome of the experiment.

Here at the end, Herod's plan of action is put into the supernatural framework of the Book of Acts as a whole, where God is the chief actor and where the great conflict between good and evil is more than earthly and human. Suddenly the story takes on the coloring of the holy war in Old Testament Israelite history, where pagan kings are portrayed as God's enemies. We notice also the appearance of an angel in these verses, another link with the story of Peter's rescue. The angel appeared to Peter and smote him to initiate deliverance; he smites Herod to initiate judgment. Similarly, Peter had earlier dressed for a rescue, whereas Herod dresses for a condemnation.

The picture that Luke draws of Herod in these verses may have been influenced by his familiarity with Greek tragedy. Greek tragedy is always about a powerful figure, usually a king, who is guilty of some great flaw of character. In Greek tragedy, moreover, this flaw is almost always some form of *hubris*, or overweening pride. God-like pride is the most acute form. It was a spectacle that moved the ancient Greeks deeply, and here we find it in brief but vivid form. Josephus recorded the same event, but in more detail. Luke's account seems more governed by the literary pattern of tragedy than the physician's viewpoint.

In this account of a king eaten by worms, Herod becomes a physical as well as moral monstrosity, a walking piece of rotten flesh covered by a symbolic robe.

The story ends with a brief and understated counterpoint to the story of judgment that precedes it: *But the word of God grew and multiplied* (v. 24). Here, in fact, is the hidden or spiritual plot in the story of Acts—the mighty acts of God contending with forces hostile to the Christian gospel.

The narrative logic of Acts 12 is impeccable. There is no detail that does not belong to the overall action. We see here in microcosm the type of narrative artistry that permeates the entire book.

What themes, finally, emerge from this well-told story? The truth that literature conveys is often representational truth—truth to the way things are in human experience. At least four themes are embodied in the story we have been considering:

1. The reality and availability of a God who is more powerful than the threats that befall his followers.
2. The power of evil in the great spiritual warfare of the ages.
3. The smallness of human faith and expectation in the daily routine of Christian living.
4. The monstrosity of human rebellion against God and his purposes.

These realities are conveyed not as ideas, but as images—images of prison and light, an open gate and a closed door, a maid named Rhoda, and royal robes glittering with gold over rotten flesh.

The story of Peter's rescue epitomizes the Book of Acts. It is an adventure story that combines everyday realism with a miracle. The story features the heroic character Peter and is a chapter in the ongoing struggle between the early Christian church and its opponents. The artistry with which the story is told is amazing.

5

The Epistles

The letter or epistle is such an amorphous literary category that it would be hard to define the conventional form by which to measure specific examples. Letters exist on a continuum in terms of their content and purpose. At the expository end we find letters intended for the utilitarian purpose of conveying information. At the other end of the spectrum we find letters that go beyond this practical purpose and assume literary qualities. The literary term *epistle* is normally reserved for letters that lean toward this end of the continuum. Often they are written with publication or at least oral reading in view.

Further categories also show the letter or epistle to be elusive. There is no determined subject matter that would help us to define the genre. Letters can tend toward either the private or public direction, with respect to both writer and audience, and these distinctions apply to both expository letters and literary epistles. Given the range of available options, writers of literary epistles are free to follow their own designs, and the resulting letters will inevitably be somewhat distinctive.

Biblical scholarship has generally taken letter writing in the ancient Greco-Roman world as a model by which to describe the New Testament epistles.[1] The conclusions support my own approach in this chapter: the New Testament epistles are rooted in familiar conventions of letter writing in the ancient world but also show many original features. In terms of content, Greek and Roman letters tended to be informational and expository, and virtually every subject can be found among these letters. The basic purpose was to exchange information between two people. The language tended to be stereotyped. The basic structure consisted of three parts—introduction (salutation and greetings), text or body, and conclusion (final wish, greetings, or prayers).

Conventional Features of the Epistles

If we compare the New Testament epistles with their Hellenistic counterparts, we find that they follow the familiar conventions in their broad outlines. At the level of content, they serve the familiar purposes of conveying information and maintaining personal acquaintance. Their opening and closing formulas resemble those in other letters of the ancient world.

They also show the usual range of formality and informality. In the New Testament epistles we find personal notes and news. Sections of travelogue are common in Paul's letters. The person addressed in New Testament letters is often an acquaintance. But we also find letters with a public, formal tone addressed to groups of people, some of whom the sender did not know personally. Some of the letters are private communications, while others were intended for oral reading and circulation (the forerunner of our "open letter" intended for publication).

Equally conventional is the occasional nature of the New Testament epistles. The Epistles are not essays. They are letters addressed to specific people and situations. Taken together, they give us a realistic picture of the varied life of the early Christian church.

It would be wrong, therefore, to regard the Epistles as systematic and expository. One scholar has described their occasional nature thus:

> Since these are letters, the points argued and stressed are often not those of the greatest importance. They are usually points about which differences of opinion existed.... The churches addressed ... knew [the author's] views on the great central facts; these he can take for granted. It is to show them their mistakes in the application of these central facts

1. See especially William G. Doty, *Letters in Primitive Christianity*, Guides to Biblical Scholarship: New Testament series, ed. Dan Otto Via, Jr. (Philadelphia: Fortress, 1973); and Leland Ryken, ed., *The New Testament in Literary Criticism*, A Library of Literary Criticism (New York: Ungar, 1984), pp. 66–77, 273–81.

to their daily life, to help their doubts, that he writes. . . . Many of the questions he discusses are those propounded by the perplexed church. He answers the question because it has been raised.[2]

Like letters generally, the New Testament epistles (with the exceptions of Romans and Hebrews) are not systematic arguments. Instead the writers assume an epistolary context in which they respond to the actual situations of their audiences. Like other letters, the epistles allude to a context.

Distinctive Features of the Epistles

If the New Testament epistles are in many ways conventional for their era, what makes them distinctive? They are more thoroughly religious and more literary in technique than most Hellenistic letters were, as the following discussion will suggest.

The Religious Emphasis

At the level of content, the New Testament epistles are almost completely theological and moral. They are very similar to the Gospels in their basic content. The concern with doctrinal truth and moral living is identical in both genres. It is this preoccupation with doctrinal and moral issues that has made the letters seem more systematic than they really are.

The religious orientation of the Epistles gave rise to innovations of form. One of these is the strongly oral cast of the Epistles. They are sermonic or homiletic in tone and style. Their writers were orators and preachers. The Epistles are accordingly full of impassioned pleading. The note of direct address to an assembled audience pervades the more public epistles. The element of confrontation is prominent.

The religious content of the Epistles also resulted in modifications of the conventional structure of the letter. While retaining the three basic elements of the ordinary letter, the New Testament epistolary form features two other significant elements, as table 1 shows at a glance.

The most notable difference is the addition of two items in the New Testament epistles, but even the conventional elements are modified in these epistles. In Paul's letters, for example, the conventional Greek formula for the salutation ("Greetings!") becomes the theologically charged "grace and peace." Whereas the subject matter covered in the body of a conventional letter might be virtually anything, the focus of

2. Morton Scott Enslin, *The Literature of the Christian Movement* (New York: Harper and Row, 1938), p. 214.

Table 1 **Epistolary form**

Hellenistic Letters	New Testament Epistles
Opening (sender, addressee, greeting)	Opening (sender, addressee, greeting)
	Thanksgiving (prayer for spiritual welfare and remembrance or commendation of the spiritual riches of the addressee)
Body	Body
	Paraenesis (exhortations)
Closing (greetings and final wishes)	Closing (final greetings and benediction)

the New Testament epistles is single-mindedly on theological and moral issues. The concluding benediction gives the conventional closing a warmly spiritual note:

> Peace be to the brethren, and love with faith, from God the Father and the Lord Jesus Christ. Grace be with all who love our Lord Jesus Christ with love undying. [Eph. 6:23–24]

The most innovative element in the New Testament epistles was the inclusion of a thanksgiving and a section of moral exhortations. The thanksgiving is a liturgically formulated statement of thanks and praise for spiritual blessings. In Paul's epistles, these thanksgivings often become small essays in the grand style. The thanksgiving in Second Thessalonians is briefer and simpler than most:

> We are bound to give thanks to God always for you, brethren, as is fitting, because your faith is growing abundantly, and the love of every one of you for one another is increasing. Therefore we ourselves boast of you in the churches of God for your steadfastness and faith in all your persecutions and in the afflictions which you are enduring. [1:3–4]

The section of moral commands, technically called *paraenesis*, is another innovation of the New Testament epistle. It is built around such motifs as proverbial wisdom, lists of vices and virtues, catalogues of commands, and extended exhortations on a single moral topic. Here is a brief specimen:

> Therefore, putting away falsehood, let every one speak the truth with his neighbor, for we are members one of another. Be angry but do not sin; do not let the sun go down on your anger, and give no opportunity to the devil. Let the thief no longer steal, but rather let him labor. . . . Let no evil talk come out of your mouths, but only such as is good for edifying. . . . [Eph. 4:25–29]

The paraenesis normally comes after the doctrinal middle section of an epistle. When we reach this moment in an epistle, we are conscious that a pivot has been made. Here is a typical transition from the doctrinal section to the moral exhortations:

> I appeal to you therefore, brethren, by the mercies of God, to present your bodies as a living sacrifice, holy and acceptable to God. . . . [Rom. 12:1]

Even when the pivot is not as clearly marked as this, the general movement of a New Testament epistle is from doctrinal instruction to moral application.

Literary Techniques

If the Epistles are more religiously oriented than most other ancient letters were, they are also more literary. They are literary first of all by virtue of how they accentuate their own set of conventions or artifice. The elaborate structural patterns that I have just noted prove that these epistles were not randomly composed. The writers were following an established genre of letter writing. To fill out the categories in the expected way and the standard order required self-conscious artistry on the part of the writers.

In addition to falling within the overall epistolary genre, the New Testament letters incorporate distinctly literary genres within them. One of these is the saying or proverb, with the most extended collection of proverbs occurring in the Epistle of James. Brief liturgical statements and creedal affirmations are also embedded in some of the Epistles. Usually a formal introduction and parallel construction will identify such units, as in Ephesians 5:14:

> Therefore it is said,
>
>> "Awake, O sleeper, and arise from the dead,
>> and Christ shall give you light."

We also find lyric poems or hymns incorporated into the Epistles, and they, too, advertise themselves by their poetic parallelism.[3] A famous example is 1 Timothy 3:16:

> Great, indeed, we confess, is the mystery of our religion:
>
>> He was manifested in the flesh,
>> vindicated in the Spirit,
>>> seen by angels,
>> preached among the nations,
>> believed on in the world,
>>> taken up in glory.

---

3. For more on the liturgical and hymnic genres in the Epistles, see *The New Testament in Literary Criticism,* pp. 142–46, and chapter 6 of this book.

The style of the Epistles is as literary as their generic traits. For example, the style is very poetic. The leading manifestation of this poetic impulse is the prevalence of concrete images and metaphors, as in Peter's portrait of false teachers:

> These are waterless springs and mists driven by a storm. . . . They themselves are slaves of corruption; for whatever overcomes a man, to that he is enslaved. . . . It has happened to them according to the true proverb, The dog turns back to his own vomit, and the sow is washed only to wallow in the mire. [2 Peter 2:17, 19, 22]

The Epistles, for all their theology, appeal continually to our imagination. We cannot get their meaning without analyzing metaphors and similes. As P. C. Sands puts it, Paul's diction "is continually enlivened by metaphor, '*glueing* yourselves to the good', '*boiling* with the spirit', '*buying up* the opportunity', 'let the love of Christ *make its home* in you', let the peace of Christ *be umpire* in your hearts'. . . ."[4]

Other figures of speech also make the style of the Epistles continuously poetic and literary. We find paradox, as when Paul writes that Christians are treated

> as imposters, and yet are true;
> as unknown, and yet well known;
> as dying, and behold we live;
> as punished, and yet not killed;
> as sorrowful, yet always rejoicing;
> as poor, yet making many rich;
> as having nothing, and yet possessing everything. [2 Cor. 6:8–10]

Equally poetic in such a passage is the elaborate parallelism of the lines.

Other poetic touches are also present. We find rhetorical questions that draw us into their orb and move us toward assent:

> If God is for us, who is against us? He who did not spare his own Son but gave him up for us all, will he not also give us all things with him? [Rom. 8:31–32]

Dramatic apostrophes are also one of the affective forms found in the Epistles: "O death, where is thy victory?" (1 Cor. 15:55). There are some memorable personifications, including James's statement that "desire when it has conceived gives birth to sin; and sin when it is full-grown brings forth death" (1:15). We also find question-and-answer constructions for dramatic effect:

4. P. C. Sands, *Literary Genius of the New Testament* (New York: Oxford University Press, 1932), p. 153.

What then? Are we to sin because we are not under law but under grace? By no means! [Rom. 6:15]

The Epistles of course share the aphoristic tendency of the whole Bible. In keeping with the practice of the Old Testament wisdom teachers and Jesus, the writers of the Epistles fill their letters with concise, memorable statements: *we are more than conquerors through him who loved us* (Rom. 8:37); *the greatest of these is love* (1 Cor. 13:13); *be doers of the word, and not hearers only* (James 1:22).

Finally, the Epistles are consistently literary, not only in their figurative language and proverbial style, but also in their highly patterned rhetoric. This artistry consists of repetition, balance, antithesis, and parallelism. Almost any page from the Epistles will illustrate this conscious design. To get the full effect, we need to print the phrases and clauses like poetry. Printed thus, the wavelike motion of the prose style is truly affecting:

> There is one body
>   and one Spirit,
> just as you were called
>   to the one hope
>   that belongs to your call,
> one Lord,
> one faith,
> one baptism,
> one God and Father of us all,
>   who is above all
>   and through all
>   and in all. [Eph. 4:4–6]

The effect of such a passage is incantatory, with the parallelism of the clauses reinforcing the repetition of the key words *one* and *all*.

Here is another memorable specimen out of many that might be quoted:

> Finally, brethren,
>   whatever is true,
>   whatever is honorable,
>   whatever is just,
>   whatever is pure,
>   whatever is lovely,
>   whatever is gracious,
> if there is any excellence,
>   if there is anything worthy of praise,
> think about these things. [Phil. 4:8]

Antithesis is a marked characteristic of Paul's mindset and world view. He perceives the world as a battleground between good and evil, God and Satan. There is, moreover, the tension between this world and the spiritual world. Paul's rhetoric is the natural vehicle for his outlook:

> What is sown is perishable,
>   what is raised is imperishable.
> It is sown in dishonor,
>   it is raised in glory.
> It is sown in weakness,
>   it is raised in power.
> It is sown a physical body,
>   it is raised a spiritual body. [1 Cor. 15:42–44]

To illustrate the combination of parallelism and antithesis that is Paul's trademark, the conclusion to Romans 8 will suffice (vv. 38–39):

> For I am sure that neither death,
>   nor life,
>   nor angels,
>   nor principalities,
>   nor things present,
>   nor things to come,
>   nor powers,
>   nor height,
>   nor depth,
>   nor anything else in all creation,
>   will be able to separate us
>   from the love of God
>   in Christ Jesus our Lord.

The exalted and highly patterned style in such a passage is not simply an embellishment. It is part of the meaning. The Epistles are affective as well as intellectual. Their style conveys an ecstasy and an emotional conviction that are an important part of their meaning.

Even the customary salutation of a letter becomes transformed into something grand and eloquent in the New Testament epistles:

> Paul, a servant of Jesus Christ,
>   called to be an apostle,
>   set apart for the gospel of God
> which he promised beforehand
>   through his prophets
>   in the holy scriptures,

the gospel concerning his Son,
  who was descended from David
  according to the flesh
and designated Son of God in power
  according to the Spirit of holiness
  by his resurrection from the dead,
Jesus Christ our Lord,
  through whom we have received grace and apostleship
to bring about the obedience of faith
  for the sake of his name
  among all the nations,
  including yourselves
  who are called to belong to Jesus Christ;
To all God's beloved in Rome,
  who are called to be saints:
Grace to you and peace
  from God our Father
  and the Lord Jesus Christ. [Rom. 1:1–7]

We have heard too much about the "unliterary" quality of the New Testament. Even if in the original the vocabulary tends to be that of ordinary speech, there is no way in which we can consider the rhetorical patterning of clauses to be ordinary.

The New Testament epistles represent a mingling of the traditional and the innovative. Like ordinary letters, they exist to convey information to an audience and are prompted by a specific occasion. Their religious focus makes them distinctive. They also differ from other ancient letters by being more consistently literary in their form and style, but this very quality makes them similar to other literature and actually enhances their accessibility for a modern reader.

6

Poetry, Proverb, and Hymn

In this chapter I am not concerned so much with specific books of the New Testament as with some general literary qualities that pervade the New Testament. I will have fulfilled my aim if I alert my readers to these general tendencies.

Poetry

When I speak of poetry in the New Testament I refer to the prevalence of concrete images and figurative language. It is a commonplace that poets speak a language all their own.[1] The language of the New Testament is often poetic.

Poetic Language

The most basic poetic unit is the image that names a concrete object or sensation. Such imagery requires of a reader the ability to *imagine* as much as possible. Poetic language is based on the premise that we can picture the truth as well as conceptualize it. Images also tend to be an *affective* medium.

---

1. For a more complete analysis of poetic language than I attempt here, see chapter 7 of my companion volume to this book, *Words of Delight: A Literary Introduction to the Bible* (Grand Rapids: Baker, 1987).

The next most prevalent ingredients in poetic language are metaphor and simile. Both compare one thing to another. A simile does so by announcing the comparison with the formula *like* or *as:* "the kingdom of heaven is like treasure hidden in a field" (Matt. 13:44). Metaphor is also a comparison, but it adopts a bolder strategy by dropping the comparative formula and simply asserting that one thing *is* another: "you are the light of the world" (Matt. 5:14).

Briefly stated, metaphor and simile require the following interpretive actions from us. They first require us to identify and experience the literal level of the comparison. Before we determine how the kingdom of God is like hidden treasure or a Christian like light, we need to experience the phenomena of treasure and light. Having experienced the phenomenon at the literal level, we need to carry over the appropriate meaning(s) to the subject that is being discussed. The very word *metaphor* suggests what we need to do. It is based on the Greek words *meta*, meaning "over," and *pherein*, meaning "to carry." With metaphor and simile, we need to *carry over* meaning from one subject to another.

Simile and metaphor assert a correspondence between two things. It is up to the reader to discover what the correspondence is (and it might be multiple). Metaphor and simile are obviously meditative forms that ask us to ponder how one thing is like another.

A number of other figures of speech fill out the poet's repertoire. A *symbol* is a concrete image or event that represents meanings in addition to itself. An *allusion* is a reference to past literature or history. *Apostrophe* consists of addressing someone or something absent as though it were present and is usually a sign of strong feeling on the part of the speaker. *Personification* occurs when a writer or speaker attributes human qualities to something nonhuman. *Hyperbole* is conscious exaggeration for the sake of effect, usually emotional effect. Most figurative speech is based on the premise of *poetic license*, meaning that the poet departs from fact to achieve an effect.

Parallelism

Most poetry is written in a discernible verse form. In the Bible, this verse form is called *parallelism*. It consists of two or more phrases that express an idea in different words but in similar grammatical form. With *synonymous parallelism*, two or more lines express a truth in the same grammatical form:

> Ask, and it will be given you;
> seek, and you will find;
> knock, and it will be opened to you. [Matt. 7:7]

With *antithetic parallelism*, the second unit introduces a contrast:

> all things were made through him,
>> and without him was not anything made that was made. [John 1:3]

Synthetic [or growing] parallelism consists of a two-line unit in which the second line simply completes the meaning of the first:

> Blessed are the poor in spirit,
>> for theirs is the kingdom of heaven. [Matt. 5:3]

In *stairstep parallelism*, the last key word in a line becomes the first main word in the next line:

> In him was *life*,
>> and the *life* was the *light* of men.
> The *light* shines in the *darkness*,
>> and the *darkness* has not overcome it. [John 1:4–5]

Several functions are served when an utterance falls into poetic rhythm. Parallelism beautifies a passage by adding artistry to it. Parallelism also heightens the impact of a statement. It has an aphoristic quality and makes a statement memorable. It focuses our attention and creates a sense of compulsion. Furthermore, emotional utterances have a natural tendency to be more rhythmical than ordinary speech. Sometimes parallelism identifies a passage as being a poem or hymn, and it always implies a certain formality. Overall, parallelism helps to produce the effect of heightened speech.

Poetry in the New Testament

Why all this talk about poetry? Because the New Testament is continuously poetic in the ways I have noted. This is somewhat obscured from us because most of it is printed as prose. But there is nothing to prevent speakers or writers from using figurative language in prose, and whenever they do, their statements require that we interpret them poetically. As I will show in a later chapter, the Book of Revelation is continuously poetic. It communicates the truth about the spiritual world and the future by means of evocative images and symbols. The Epistles are not this continuously figurative, but we certainly cannot interpret their message without knowing how to interpret figures of speech at many points as we read. Verses like this abound: "I beseech you as aliens and exiles to abstain from the passions of the flesh that wage war against your soul" (1 Peter 2:11).

As for parallelism, much more of the New Testament should be printed in poetic lines than is usually done. Regardless of how we print it, much of it is couched in parallel clauses:

> Let every man be quick to hear, slow to speak, slow to anger. [James 1:19]

> When I was a child, I spoke like a child, I thought like a child, I reasoned like a child. [1 Cor. 13:11]

> Worthy is the Lamb who was slain, to receive power and wealth and wisdom and might and honor and glory and blessing! [Rev. 5:12]

> Whoever receives this child in my name receives me, and whoever receives me receives him who sent me. [Luke 9:48]

The flow of clauses and phrases in the New Testament is often rhythmic in this way, and as such its effect can appropriately be called poetic.

Jesus as Poet

The leading poet of the New Testament is of course Jesus.[2] In fact, Jesus is one of the world's most famous poets. His sermons and discourses are essentially poetic in style.

Jesus' speech, for example, is saturated with metaphors and similes, as he repeatedly uses one area of human experience to cast light on another area. Calling people to belief in God is like gathering a harvest (Matt. 9:37–38). Sending the disciples to minister in a hostile world is similar to sending "sheep in the midst of wolves" (Matt. 10:16). Living a life of self-sacrifice for the sake of Christ becomes a picture of someone picking up a cross and bearing it (Matt. 10:38), while the ordeal of Jesus' own death is a cup whose contents must be drunk (Matt. 26:39).

Jesus compared the hypocritical Pharisees to "whitewashed tombs, which outwardly appear beautiful, but within . . . are full of dead men's bones and all uncleanness" (Matt. 23:27), and to "graves which are not seen, and men walk over them without knowing it" (Luke 11:44). Many of Jesus' comparisons are archetypal symbols, as when he speaks about living water (John 4:10), the bread of life (John 6:35), the light of the world (John 8:12), and the good shepherd (John 10:11). Jesus' reliance on analogy as the most effective way to explain his saving ministry reaches its climax in the parables, where the kingdom of God is compared to such things as a field, a mustard seed, a treasure, a pearl, a vineyard, a banquet, and a wedding.

Jesus also used bold paradoxes to startle his listeners. He spoke of

---

2. For more commentary on Jesus as poet, see the selections in Leland Ryken, ed., *The New Testament in Literary Criticism*, A Library of Literary Criticism (New York: Ungar, 1984), pp. 152–63.

a burden that was light (Matt. 11:30), of saving one's life by losing it (Matt. 16:25), of the first being last and the last first (Mark 10:31). Such paradoxes are not merely rhetorical devices; they are essential to Jesus' message. From start to finish, Jesus came to subvert conventional ways of thinking. The language of the gospel is shocking because the coming of Christ's kingdom reverses earthly standards of value. In Jesus' teaching, a revolutionary message naturally produced its own revolutionary discourse.

This explains another characteristic feature of Jesus' speech, his use of hyperbole or exaggeration. Elton Trueblood calls it the giantesque motif.[3] The most famous example is Jesus' statement that "it is easier for a camel to go through the eye of a needle than for a rich man to enter the kingdom of God" (Matt. 19:24). On a par is the satiric picture of the Pharisees "straining out a gnat and swallowing a camel" (23:24). And then there is the hilarious picture of someone wildly swinging a log from his own eye while claiming to be able to get a speck of dirt out of someone else's eye (Luke 6:42).

Such overstatements are of course not intended to be taken literally. Jesus was not stating a reasoned ethical position when he said that "if any one comes to me and does not hate his own father and mother and wife and children and brothers and sisters, yes, and even his own life, he cannot be my disciple" (Luke 14:26). He was using hyperbole to assert the priority that a person must give to God over other relationships.

The speech of Jesus was essentially poetic. He spoke in images rather than theological abstractions. He thought in pictures. As Oliver Cromwell put it, Jesus spoke *things*. When we read the words of Jesus, we are not in a world of systematic theology but in a world of everyday objects—of chickens and lilies and lamps. To understand the message of Jesus in the Gospels, we need to apply all that we know about how poetry works.

Proverb

In addition to being poetic, the New Testament is also proverbial or aphoristic.[4] An aphorism is a concise, memorable statement of truth. Like poetry, it is heightened speech and requires a skill with words

3. Elton Trueblood, *The Humor of Christ* (New York: Harper and Row, 1964), p. 47. This is the topic that Trueblood handles most expertly in his small classic.

4. For commentary on the proverb as a New Testament form, see the excerpts collected in *The New Testament in Literary Criticism*, pp. 295–301; and Robert C. Tannehill, *The Sword of His Mouth: Forceful and Imaginative Language in Synoptic Sayings* (Philadelphia: Fortress, 1975).

that most people lack. In both form and content, the proverbial literature of the New Testament shows affinities to Old Testament wisdom literature, which in biblical times was both folk literature and a form of instruction.

The Sayings of Jesus

When we think of proverbial literature in the New Testament, we naturally think first of the sayings of Jesus. Even more of Jesus' teaching is encapsulated in his sayings than in his parables. Everywhere we turn in the Gospels, the words of Jesus fall continuously into the concise, chiseled form of proverbs that are almost impossible to forget: "a prophet is not without honor, except in his own country" (Mark 6:4); "no one can serve two masters" (Matt. 6:24); "where your treasure is, there will your heart be also" (Luke 12:34). Many of Jesus' sayings have passed into the storehouse of common proverbs.

Proverbs have a power beyond that of ordinary speech. They are a product of the literary imagination. Perhaps this explains why the proverbs of Jesus often merge with figurative language. Many of them make use of metaphor: "you are the salt of the earth" (Matt. 5:13); "I am the vine, you are the branches" (John 15:5). Some of Jesus' proverbs depend on hyperbole for their impact: "when you give alms, do not let your left hand know what your right hand is doing" (Matt. 6:3). Other proverbs are based on paradox: "whoever would save his life will lose it" (Mark 8:35). Still others reinforce the compelling effect of proverbs with a rhetorical question: "for what does it profit a man, to gain the whole world and forfeit his life?" (Mark 8:36).

In these specimens we can catch the subversive quality of Jesus' sayings. In the Old Testament, proverbs tend to be statements of worldly wisdom that reinforce conventional religious thinking. They do not shock our sensibilities. To be told that "a good man obtains favor from the Lord, / but a man of evil devices he condemns" (Prov. 12:2) confirms what a religious person already believes. But the sayings of Jesus often challenge conventional thinking. They reverse ordinary expectations and therefore employ such speech patterns as paradox and hyperbole. Their goal is to jolt us into a new judgment about values and ourselves.

Another reason proverbs occur frequently in the Gospels is that they are often linked with narratives and parables, so that we remember event and saying together. One of the subtypes in the Gospels is the pronouncement story in which a saying of Jesus is paired with an event that it explains or illustrates:

> And as he sat at table in his house, many tax collectors and sinners were sitting with Jesus and his disciples. . . . And the scribes of the Phar-

isees . . . said to his disciples, "Why does he eat with tax collectors and sinners?" And when Jesus heard it, he said to them, "Those who are well have no need of a physician, but those who are sick; I came not to call the righteous, but sinners." [Mark 2:15–17]

Even when a Gospel unit is not primarily a pronouncement story, the sayings of Jesus are often part of the episode. The story of the woman taken in adultery, for example, is a conflict story, but in the middle of the account Jesus utters a memorable proverb: "Let him who is without sin among you be the first to throw a stone at her" (John 8:7).

As with the narrative parts of the Gospels, so with the parables. They are often preceded and/or followed by an aphorism of Jesus. The parable of the marriage feast, for example, ends with the proverb, "For every one who exalts himself will be humbled, and he who humbles himself will be exalted" (Luke 14:11). In addition to these aphorisms surrounding the parables, much of the actual parabolic material is phrased in such a memorable way that we can call it aphoristic: "Go out to the highways and hedges, and compel people to come in, that my house may be filled" (Luke 14:23).

Proverbs in the Epistles

The second great repository of proverbs in the New Testament is the Epistles. The style of Paul, for example, is marked by an epigrammatic tendency: "the wages of sin is death, but the free gift of God is eternal life in Christ Jesus our Lord" (Rom. 6:23); "the love of money is the root of all evils" (1 Tim. 6:10); "for to me to live is Christ, and to die is gain" (Phil. 1:21). Sometimes Paul incorporates an existing proverb into his writing: "a little leaven leavens the whole lump" (Gal. 5:9; 1 Cor. 5:6); "bad company ruins good morals" (1 Cor. 15:33).

Throughout the Epistles we note a tendency to include proverbial sayings; the Epistle of James as a whole falls into the genre of wisdom literature. The very structure of this epistle—a series of small, self-contained units that follow each other in rapid-fire succession—is that of wisdom literature. The subject matter—practical Christian morality—is likewise what we expect in wisdom literature. Everywhere we find the aphoristic gift of stating the truth with memorable terseness: "be doers of the word, and not hearers only" (1:22); "draw near to God and he will draw near to you" (4:8).

A common strategy in biblical wisdom literature is to draw extensively upon the world of nature for similes and analogies to human behavior. The Epistle of James makes frequent use of the technique:

If we put bits into the mouths of horses that they may obey us, we guide their whole bodies. Look at the ships also; though they are so great and are driven by strong winds, they are guided by a very small rudder wherever the will of the pilot directs. So the tongue is a little member and boasts of great things. How great a forest is set ablaze by a small fire! And the tongue is a fire. [3:3–6]

Part of the genius of wisdom literature like this is its ability to put us in touch with ordinary human experience. The proverbs of the New Testament are one of the things that make the New Testament a book of the people.

Interpreting Proverbs

The proverbial nature of much of the New Testament requires that we know how to interpret proverbs. It is important to note in the first place that the proverb is *a meditative form*. It invites us to pause and consider it carefully. It is very much an oral form, which perhaps helps to explain why Jesus chose it so consistently for his discourses. He wanted to give his hearers something to ponder as they left him. Nor should we forget that the disciples who followed Jesus were the designated recorders of Jesus' teaching after his death—recorders for whom memory was crucial in their preaching and composition of the Gospels.

The important principle of interpretation that follows from this is that *a proverb does not put an end to thought on a subject*. It is designed rather to stimulate further thought and application. Its very terseness helps to insure that we will take note of it. A good proverb is so striking that it not only expresses an insight but compels it. Those who hear or read a proverb, writes a biblical scholar, "receive it somewhat in the way one receives a curious object which one must examine in order to find out how it can be used. They are given a text upon which they can ruminate and discuss with one another in an effort to clarify its meaning."[5]

A second rule for interpreting a proverb is to realize that it states *a universal principle about life*. A proverb is an insight into the repeatable situations of life. This means that proverbs are open-ended in their application to life. This is part of their inexhaustibility. The proverb that "whatever a man sows, that he will also reap" (Gal. 6:7) applies to many situations of life. The truth that "men loved darkness rather than light" (John 3:19) is always being confirmed by our observations of life. Part of interpreting a proverb is therefore to ponder what it means and how it applies. Proverbs organize our understand-

5. Birger Gerhardsson, *The Origins of the Gospel Tradition*, in *The New Testament in Literary Criticism*, p. 156.

ing of reality, but we have to supply the data from experience that they organize.

A third thing to note about the proverbs of the New Testament is that they *are often figurative rather than literal.* I noted that proverbs often use the resources of metaphor, simile, paradox, and hyperbole. When they do, we need to apply all that we know about interpreting figurative language. When Jesus says, "My yoke is easy, and my burden is light" (Matt. 11:30), he uses metaphor and paradox rather than literal statement and requires us to interpret them.

Finally, we will do a better job of interpreting proverbs if we realize the impulse behind them. Proverbs are part of *the human urge for order.* Proverbial thinking enables us to master the complexity of life by bringing human experience under the control of an observation that explains it and unifies many similar experiences. Proverbs are a way of organizing what we know to be true of life. A New Testament scholar expresses it thus: "The essence of a proverbial saying is that it is based on observation of how things are in the world. . . . In the context of a firm belief in God, the proverb comes to express insight into the way things are, or should be, in the world ordered by God and a challenge to behaviour that God will reward."[6] New Testament proverbs are high points of insight into reality—moments of spiritual focus in which we see life clearly in God's terms.

New Testament Hymns

In the New Testament, poetic language and proverbs do not exist by themselves but are intermingled with the prose that is the dominant form. The same is true of the lyric quality that I discuss in this section. Prose and poetry, narrative and lyric, are not kept separate in the New Testament. Lyric poetry is mingled with narrative in the Gospels and the Book of Revelation, and with expository prose in the Epistles, where the prose itself often becomes lyrical.

Lyrical discourse is either meditative/reflective or emotional/affective in nature. It is writing that creates a mood and often has a singing quality. It is intense, unified, compressed, and highly patterned. Often it is poetic in its use of images and regular rhythm (in the Bible, parallelism). Lyric is heightened speech and is always *a response* to the subject about which the speaker or writer speaks.

This lyric *quality* is pervasive in the New Testament epistles and

6. Norman Perrin, *The New Testament: An Introduction* (New York: Harcourt Brace Jovanovich, 1974), p. 296.

the Book of Revelation. As an example of the former, here is Paul's charged description of the confidence that comes to those who have been saved by Christ:

> What then shall we say to this? If God is for us, who is against us? He who did not spare his own Son but gave him up for us all, will he not also give us all things with him? Who shall bring any charge against God's elect? It is God who justifies; who is to condemn? Is it Christ Jesus, who died, yes, who was raised from the dead, who is at the right hand of God, who indeed intercedes for us? Who shall separate us from the love of Christ? Shall tribulation, or distress, or persecution, or famine, or nakedness, or peril, or sword? . . . No, in all these things we are more than conquerors through him who loved us. [Rom. 8:31–37]

A similar ecstasy is just below the surface in the Book of Revelation, where the true lyric voice often asserts itself:

> To him who loves us and has freed us from our sins by his blood and made us a kingdom, priests to his God and Father, to him be glory and dominion for ever and ever. Amen. [1:5–6]

In addition to this general lyric *quality*, the New Testament possesses a number of lyric *genres*. The purpose of the discussion that follows is to identify these genres and to offer a few critical comments that I leave my readers to develop.

Nativity Hymns

Passages of lyric poetry alternate with narrative in the account of the annunciation and birth of Christ in Luke's Gospel. One of these lyrics is the Magnificat (so called after the opening word of its Latin translation) of Mary in Luke 1:46–55. Modeled on the Old Testament psalm of praise and more specifically on the song of Hannah (1 Sam. 2:1–10), the hymn unfolds as a catalogue of God's acts of grace to Mary herself (vv. 48–53) and to the nation of Israel (vv. 54–55).

The Benedictus (also named after its Latin opening) of Zechariah (Luke 1:68–79) likewise has two parts. The first (vv. 68–75) praises God for having fulfilled his promises to his people Israel. The second half (vv. 76–79) is an address to Zechariah's own infant child John the Baptist. The hymn combines the retrospect of Old Testament prophecy with the prospect of fulfillment in the immediate future.

The nativity itself is also accompanied by songs. One is the song of the angels to the shepherds (Luke 2:14). Another is the song of Simeon in the temple (Luke 2:29–32), which is a brief version of the same motifs as the song of Zechariah had developed.

Poetic Fragments Used in Worship

When we move to the Epistles, we find brief poetic passages that modern scholars believe were part of early Christian worship. Leaving aside some of the overly speculative and ingenious attempts to find hymns in the New Testament, there remain stylistic criteria for discerning poetic or liturgical passages. These criteria include introductory or concluding formulas that identify a passage as confessional or hymnic, the presence of parallelism or other unusual grammatical features, a pronounced rhythmical and/or lyric quality, and poetic vocabulary.

Ephesians 5:14 illustrates these features:

Therefore it is said,

> "Awake, O sleeper,
> and arise from the dead,
> and Christ shall give you light."

The formula in the first line identifies the utterance as one that is commonly repeated in Christian circles. By being couched as a direct address to a generalized Christian audience ("O sleeper"), the statement uses the poetic device of apostrophe. In addition to this bit of poetic license, the lines contain parallel clauses, as well as metaphors (sleep, death, light). This imagery leads most scholars to claim that this brief passage is a hymn or chant used in early Christian baptism services.

Hymnic criteria are met in 2 Timothy 2:11–13 as well:

The saying is sure:

> If we have died with him,
>   we shall also live with him;
> if we endure,
>   we shall also reign with him;
> if we deny him,
>   he also will deny us;
> if we are faithless,
>   he remains faithful—
> for he cannot deny himself.

Scholars who are familiar with the original Greek of the New Testament place Hebrews 1:3 in the same category:

> He reflects the glory of God
>   and bears the very stamp of his nature,
> upholding the universe
>   by his word of power.

In the Greek, 1 Peter 1:18–21 and 2:21–25 also qualify.

Sometimes a passage that seems like ordinary prose is accompanied by a formula that suggests that the passage may have been a liturgical unit. For example, Titus 3:5–7 is followed by the statement *the saying is sure* (v. 8). Similarly, Titus 2:11–14 is followed by the comment *declare these things* (v. 15).

Hymns in the Book of Revelation

The Book of Revelation, in which the main impulse is to exalt the work of Christ, contains numerous lyric fragments. They are identifiable by their parallelism and lyric content. Their subject is usually adoration, and the context in which they appear is ordinarily heavenly worship. The fourth chapter of Revelation contains two examples:

> Holy, holy, holy, is the Lord God Almighty,
> who was and is and is to come! [v. 8]

> Worthy art thou, our Lord and God,
> to receive glory and honor and power,
> for thou didst create all things,
> and by thy will they existed and were created [v. 11]

Similar passages include 5:9–10; 7:12; 11:17–18; 15:3–4; and 19:1–8.

Christ Hymns

We come, finally, to a genre of New Testament lyrics that are so stylistically exalted and poetically great that they deserve a section by themselves. They are known today as Christ hymns. They are written in the verse form of parallelism and are highly patterned in their arrangement. In content, they are Christocentric and fraught with theological themes.

John 1:1–18

The prologue with which the Gospel of John opens is an encomium that praises the incarnate Christ.[7] The poem consists of eight stanzas. In this version I have used italics to draw attention to patterns of repetition within stanzas. Even more repetition emerges if one studies the whole poem to see and hear key words and phrases.

The poem begins by announcing the divine origin of Christ:

> *In the beginning* was *the Word,*
> and *the Word* was with God,
> and *the Word* was God.
> He was *in the beginning* with God.

---

7. For explications of this poem and Colossians 1:15–20 in terms of the encomium, see chapter 12 of *Words of Delight*.

When John wrote these lines, pagan Greeks had for three centuries sung Cleanthes' *Hymn to Zeus*, which also praised a divine word— "the universal Word, that flows through all, and the light celestial. . . . One Word—whose voice alas! the wicked spurn."[8] By echoing the familiar pagan vocabulary, John's poem assumes the status of a parody (a work that echoes an earlier one, but with inverted effect). What the pagans ascribed to Zeus, John attributes to Christ.

The brief second stanza uses antithetic parallelism to assert the cosmic importance of Christ:

> All things were made through him,
>> and without him was not anything made that was made.

Christ is here praised for being indispensable to the entire cosmos. To heighten the impact, the writer speaks in terms of absolute contrasts: *all things* versus *not anything, through him* versus *without him.*

The third stanza gains its eloquence through the use of stairstep parallelism:

> In him was *life*,
>> and the *life* was the *light* of men.
> The *light* shines in the *darkness*,
>> and the *darkness* has not overcome it.

Here, too, is the poetic impulse to think in images and symbols, in this case light and darkness and warfare. This is not incidental but rather integral to the total meaning of the utterance. Ralph P. Martin has written in this regard,

> It may be thought that the classification of parts of the New Testament according to the basic patterns of poetic and hymnic form is an interesting exercise but nothing more. This is not so. . . . Much of the hymnic language is poetic and suggestive of deep spiritual reality rather than prosaic and pedestrian. The early Christians . . . were seeking to interpret their understanding of God's salvation in a way which defied rational and coherent statement. Hence they had recourse to the language of symbol.[9]

8. I have quoted these brief excerpts from William M. Ramsay, *The Layman's Guide to the New Testament*, Layman's Bible Commentary series (Atlanta: John Knox, 1980), p. 243.

9. Ralph P. Martin, "Approaches to New Testament Exegesis," in *The New Testament in Literary Criticism*, pp. 145–46.

The imagery of light becomes fused with the image of kingship in the next stanza:

> There was a man sent from God,
>   whose name was John.
> He came for testimony,
>   *to bear witness* to *the light,*
>   that all might believe through him.
> He was not *the light,*
>   but came *to bear witness* to *the light.*

In ancient cultures, kings had heralds who went before them to proclaim their arrival. Here Christ is portrayed as such a king.

The fifth stanza, the longest in the poem, praises Christ's lifebringing power:

> The true light that enlightens every man
>   was coming into *the world.*
> He was in *the world,*
>   and *the world* was made through him,
>   yet *the world* knew him not.
> He came to his own home,
>   and his own people received him not.
> But to all who received him,
>   who believed in his name,
> he gave power to become children of God;
> who were born,
>   not of blood
>   nor of the will of the flesh
>   nor of the will of man,
> but of God.

The unity and coherence of the poem are amazing. Christ as light continues to be a dominant motif. Christ's creation of the world is echoed from earlier parts of the poem. So is the motif of conflict, as Christ is rejected and has to overcome the impotence of nature in order to bring people to spiritual life.

The famous sixth stanza praises the fact of the incarnation itself:

> And the Word became flesh
>   and dwelt among us,
>   full of grace and truth;
> We have beheld his glory,
>   glory as of the only Son from the Father.

Along with exalted spiritual abstractions (grace, truth, glory), we find more metaphor. Christ is a *Word* that reveals God to people. The thoroughness with which the incarnate Christ identified with humans is forced upon our consciousness when Christ is said to have *dwelt among us*.

The poem proceeds much as a piece of music does. It introduces motifs, abandons them temporarily, and then resumes them. In the seventh stanza, the poem reintroduces John the Baptist for purposes of declaring the superiority of Christ:

> (John bore witness to him, and cried,
> "This was he of whom I said,
> 'He who comes *after me* ranks *before me*,
> for he was *before me*.' ")

There is a paradoxical play on the words *after me* and *before me* in the passage. Though born after John, Christ is *before* him, by virtue of both his deity and his having been with God *in the beginning* (stanza 1).

The final stanza praises the subject of the poem by first declaring his superiority and then asserting his indispensability:

> And from his fulness have we all received,
> *grace* upon *grace*.
> For the law was given through Moses;
> *grace* and truth came through Jesus Christ.
> No one has ever seen God;
> the only Son,
> who is in the bosom of the Father,
> he has made him known.

What Christ brought to the human race is *superior* to the law that Moses brought, and Christ is the *indispensable* revealer of God to people, who cannot see God but who can know him through the incarnate Son.

This great hymn is a prime illustration of Northrop Frye's claim that "the simplicity of the Bible is the simplicity of majesty."[10] The vocabulary and syntax of the hymn are simple. The images are those of the primitive or unsophisticated imagination: light, darkness, combat, kingship, birth. Out of these simple ingredients the poet weaves a tapestry that has a moving grandeur.

10. Northrop Frye, *The Great Code: The Bible and Literature* (New York: Harcourt Brace Jovanovich, 1981), p. 211.

1 Timothy 3:16

From the grandeur of John's prologue we can move to the quiet simplicity of 1 Timothy 3:16. It has the classic form of a hymn embedded in a New Testament epistle, complete with an introductory formula and parallel construction:

> Great indeed, we confess,
>   is the mystery of our religion:
>
> He was manifested in the flesh,
>   vindicated in the Spirit,
> seen by angels,
>   preached among the nations,
> believed on in the world,
>   taken up in glory.

The poem is structured in couplets, each of which is built on the principle of contrast. The nouns that conclude the lines in the English translation are the key to this: they contrast two world orders—divine and human, heavenly and earthly. Here, in kernel form, is the essence of the incarnation itself.

Philippians 2:5–11

Philippians 2:5–11 likewise begins with a formula, this time the command, familiar in the encomium, to emulate:

> Have this mind among yourselves,
>   which is yours in Christ Jesus.

The hymn that follows consists of six stanzas that fall thematically into three movements—Christ preexistent, incarnate, and exalted.[11]
The first stanza opens the drama with Christ in heaven:

> who, though he was in the form of God,
>   did not count equality with God
>   a thing to be grasped.

The image of *grasping* in this stanza is a metaphor from the battlefield. It meant to plunder or seize a spoil of war. In its context in the poem,

---

11. For a complete treatment of the hymn and scholarship on it, see Ralph P. Martin, *Carmen Christi: Philippians 2:5–11 in Recent Interpretation and in the Setting of Early Christian Worship* (Grand Rapids: Eerdmans, 1983).

it means that Christ did not cling to his right or privilege of deity the way a soldier insists on keeping what he has won in battle.

The next two stanzas advance us from heaven to earth with their account of the incarnation itself:

> but emptied himself,
>> taking the form of a servant,
>> being born in the likeness of men.
> And being found in human form
>> he humbled himself,
>> and became obedient unto death,
>> even death on a cross.

The controlling metaphor in these two stanzas is that of the slave. The word *servant* here means a slave without rights or privileges in society. The last phrase, *even death on a cross*, belongs with this image as well, since the Romans reserved crucifixion for slaves and fomenters of revolutions.

The first half of the poem has been a downward spiral from the greatest possible height to the lowest possible depth. At this midpoint, the drama of Christ's humiliation is reversed by a corresponding ascent. First Christ is described as receiving an exalted name:

> Therefore God has highly exalted him
> and bestowed on him the name
> which is above every name.

What Christ refused to cling to or claim is now bestowed on him.

Next we catch a glimpse of the cosmic power that accompanies the exalted name:

> that at the name of Jesus every knee should bow,
>> in heaven
>> and on earth
>> and under the earth.

Here is the image of lordship that reverses the earlier servanthood.

Because a Christ hymn like this was probably part of early Christian worship, it appropriately ends on a note of confession:

> and every tongue confess
>> that Jesus Christ is Lord,
>> to the glory of God the Father.

The climax of this hymn's drama of redemption is the believer's confession that a new age has already begun.

Colossians 1:15-20

The traits of both form and content that I have noted in the Christ hymns of the New Testament are epitomized in the hymn found in Colossians 1:15–20. This Christ hymn consists of two companion poems. The first exalts Christ's supremacy over creation, while the second extols his headship over the church. The impact of companion poems depends on our tracing the parallels between the two parts. In this hymn, everything in the first poem corresponds to something in the second. In figure 2 the two poems are printed with lines that show the connections, and I leave it to my readers to ponder what those correspondences are.

The keynote of the companion poems is the idea of supremacy. The best index to this emphasis is the recurrence of the words *all* and *everything: all creation, all things* (a total of five times), *in everything, all the fulness.*

The companion poems of Colossians 1 encapsulate the New Testament forms I have discussed in this chapter. They are poetic in form. Their lines have the concise, memorable quality that we associate with the proverbial quality of New Testament literature. The passage shares the lyric quality of much of the New Testament and falls into the specific New Testament genre of the Christ hymn.

Figure 2 **Parallels within Colossians 1:15–20**

Christ over Creation	Christ over the Church

He is the image of the invisible God,
    the first-born of all creation;
	He is the head of the body,
	    the church.

for in him all things were created,
    in heaven and on earth,
    whether thrones
    or dominions
    or principalities
    or authorities—
all things were created through him
    and for him.
	He is the beginning,
	    the first-born from the dead,
	that in everything he might be preeminent.

He is before all things,
    and in him all things hold together.
	For in him all the fulness of God was
	    pleased to dwell,
	and through him to reconcile to himself all things,
	    whether on earth or in heaven,
	    making peace by the blood of his cross.

7

Oratory

Two features of New Testament literature provide the context for my treatment of oratory as a major form in the New Testament. One is the context from which the New Testament originally came. Much of the New Testament first existed in oral form. Jesus, for example, did not write his words as we find them in the Gospels. He spoke them. The Epistles and the Book of Revelation were read aloud in the churches. In cultures that relied on the spoken rather than the written word, the forms of the spoken word are prominent in the literature that is produced. To read the New Testament is to become a listener of the spoken word.

A second literary framework into which I wish to place New Testament oratory is drama. Although the New Testament is not written in the form of a play, the dramatic impulse is everywhere evident. In the narrative sections and the Book of Revelation, we are hard pressed to find pages on which we do not observe characters speaking and acting in the manner of drama. Directly quoted speeches and dialogue suffuse the New Testament, as in this typical passage:

Then they seized [Jesus] and led him away, bringing him into the high priest's house. Peter followed at a distance; and when they had kindled a fire in the middle of the courtyard and sat down together, Peter sat among them. Then a maid, seeing him as he sat in the light and gazing at him, said, "This man also was with him." But he denied it, saying, "Woman, I do not know him." And a little later some one else saw him and said, "You also are one of them." But Peter said, "Man, I am not." And after an interval of about an hour still another insisted, saying, "Certainly this man also was with him; for he is a Galilean." But Peter said, "Man, I do not know what you are saying." And immediately, while he was still speaking, the cock crowed. And the Lord turned and looked at Peter. . . . And [Peter] went out and wept bitterly. [Luke 22:54–62]

This is a drama in miniature. The characters are stationed in definite settings. Stage directions for the movements and gestures of characters are written into the script. In effect, the account begins with the familiar "enter Peter" and ends with "exit Peter." In addition, we listen to the actual dialogue in which the characters engage in their face-to-face encounters.

In this chapter I propose to look at a specific genre within the general categories of literature and drama. It is the extended formal address of a speaker to a specific audience. Such addresses comprise more of the New Testament than we may be aware. I have chosen to explicate specimens from the three main repositories of such New Testament oration. Those repositories are the discourses of Jesus recorded in the Gospels, the speeches in the Book of Acts, and the Epistles (which are often written speeches). My aim is to uncover some of the rhetorical techniques and artistry that help to give these orations their power.

Jesus' Sermon on the Mount

Jesus' Sermon on the Mount (Matt. 5–7) will illustrate the typical features of his addresses. Five of these features will be especially prominent.

One characteristic is *an aphoristic tendency*. Because a proverb stays with an audience, it lent itself to the oral nature of Jesus' sermons. After all, the proverbs of Jesus do not put an end to thought on a subject. They stimulate further thought and application.

The style of Jesus' addresses is *poetic* as well as proverbial. Jesus relies heavily on concrete imagery, metaphor, simile, paradox, and hyperbole. In addition, much of his speech falls naturally into the poetic form of Hebrew parallelism.

Recent commentators on the Gospels have also shown how *intricately patterned* the discourses of Jesus are. The key ingredient in such patterning is some form of repetition, recurrence, or balance. Here is an example of patterning on a small scale from Jesus' Olivet Discourse (Matt. 24:40–41):

> Then two men will be in the field;
>   one is taken and one is left.
> Two women will be grinding at the mill;
>   one is taken and one is left.

We will see the same impulse toward intricate patterning on a grand scale when we observe the outline of the Sermon on the Mount.

A fourth trait of Jesus' discourses is *a strong subversive element.* Jesus repeatedly assaults our patterns of deep thought and undermines our conventional way of thinking and valuing. The famous Beatitudes will highlight the tendency.

Finally, Jesus' discourses often show a literary sophistication by being *a fusion of literary genres.* The Sermon on the Mount, for example, brings together such diverse genres as the beatitude, the character sketch, proverb, satire, lyric, and parable. The sermon as a whole has affinities with utopian literature. It is an inaugural address in which Jesus outlines the principles of his ideal society, conceived as a spiritual kingdom governed by personal spirituality and morality. The sermon is also an example of wisdom literature, in which the wise authority figure sits in the middle of his disciples and instructs them.

The Structure of the Sermon

The principle of organization in Jesus' sermon is relatively simple and highly artistic. Units are either extended passages on a single topic, or fall into a threefold pattern in which three similar items are listed in succession. Here is the pattern that Jesus followed:

1. Prologue: setting and audience (5:1–2).
2. A portrait of the Christian:
   a. the Beatitudes (5:3–12);
   b. two metaphors—salt and light (5:13–16).
3. Jesus' interpretation of the Old Testament law (5:17–48).
4. Instructions on three religious observances:
   a. giving alms (6:1–4);
   b. prayer (6:5–15);
   c. fasting (6:16–18).
5. A threefold exhortation about choosing right values:
   a. choosing between earthly and heavenly treasure (6:19–21);
   b. choosing between light and darkness (6:22–23);
   c. choosing between God and mammon (6:24).

6. The discourse on not being anxious (6:25–34).
7. Instruction on three practices:
   a. judging others (7:1–5);
   b. witnessing (7:6);
   c. prayer (7:7–12).
8. Three great contrasts, or a threefold challenge to act on what Jesus has said:
   a. the wide and narrow gates (7:13–14);
   b. true and false prophets (7:15–23);
   c. the wise and foolish housebuilders (7:24–27).
9. Epilogue: the response of the crowd (7:28–29).

The artistry of the design is apparent. There is no reason why the sermon as it stands could not be exactly the form that Jesus' longer sermons took.

The Portrait of the Christian

The beatitudes that begin the sermon (5:3–12) are a character portrait of the ideal follower of Jesus. They are one of the most patterned passages in the Bible:

> [3]"Blessed are the poor in spirit,
>   for theirs is the kingdom of heaven.
> [4]Blessed are those who mourn,
>   for they shall be comforted.
> [5]Blessed are the meek,
>   for they shall inherit the earth.
> [6]Blessed are those who hunger and thirst for righteousness,
>   for they shall be satisfied.
> [7]Blessed are the merciful,
>   for they shall obtain mercy.
> [8]Blessed are the pure in heart,
>   for they shall see God.
> [9]Blessed are the peacemakers,
>   for they shall be called sons of God.
> [10]Blessed are those who are persecuted for righteousness' sake,
>   for theirs is the kingdom of heaven.
> [11]Blessed are you when men revile you and persecute you
>   and utter all kinds of evil against you falsely on my account.
> [12]Rejoice and be glad,
>   for your reward is great in heaven,
> for so men persecuted the prophets
>   who were before you."

The most obvious element of artistry is the parallelism of statements. Each beatitude follows a similar grammatical pattern consisting of three parts: an initial pronouncement of blessing (*Blessed are . . .*), the naming of a character type, and a rationale for the pronouncement of blessing (starting with the statements *for they shall* or *for theirs is*). This parallelism of expression, which comes straight from the Hebrew poetry that Jesus loved, lends an aphoristic quality to the individual beatitudes and links them with the proverbs of wisdom literature.

The subversive quality of Jesus' message also comes through strongly. For proof, we can first look at the type of person that Jesus considers happy or blessed. The character traits that Jesus names are spiritual and moral and as such run counter to conventional ideas of what makes a person happy. Once we are alerted to this spiritual orientation, we can see that the rewards that Jesus promises are likewise spiritual. In fact, they adhere to the common pattern of the beatitude in the New Testament, where beatitudes tend to be eschatological in content, pronouncing a blessing on those who will share in the coming kingdom of Christ.

To complete his portrait of the Christian, Jesus utters two of his most famous metaphors (5:13–16). God's ideal person has the preserving and flavoring influence in society that salt has with food, and the ability to reveal truth to people that a lighted lamp has in a dark room.

The Discourse About the Law

From his opening portrait of the ideal Christian Jesus moves to a long explanation of his relationship to the Jewish law (5:17–48). First we should notice the rhetorical patterning that makes the passage easy to follow. Jesus discusses six Jewish laws and follows a similar pattern in each unit. He begins with the formula, *You have heard that it was said . . .*, followed by his repetition of a familiar law. Having summarized the traditional command, Jesus counters it with his own teaching, beginning with the formula *but I say to you. . . .* The rhetorical pattern is based on a principle of antithesis.

The actual content of this passage has often been distorted. A careful look at what Jesus says shows that he is not abolishing the Old Testament moral law. In fact, he announces at the outset that "whoever then relaxes one of the least of these commandments and teaches men so, shall be called least in the kingdom of heaven" (5:19). Jesus simply calls his followers to go beyond what the moral law requires in their dealings with other people.

The law, for example, prohibited murder (5:21). But Jesus expects his followers to live by a higher morality than that. He expects them to refrain from uncontrolled anger and hatred (vv. 22–26). Again we can see the subversive nature of Jesus' message: instead of encouraging people to be satisfied with obeying the letter of the law, Jesus tells them to obey the spirit of the law as well. His theme is that "unless your righteousness exceeds that of the scribes and Pharisees, you will never enter the kingdom of heaven" (5:20).

Three Observances and Three Choices

Following the extended passage dealing with the law, Jesus moves to two sections built out of brief units. The organizing rhetorical pattern in both passages is a threefold pattern.

The first unit deals with three religious practices—giving alms (6:1–4), prayer (6:5–15), and fasting (6:16–18). Here, too, Jesus' statements fall into a rhetorical pattern of antithesis, as he contrasts ostentatious religion with religion practiced in secret. The pivot in each unit comes when Jesus concludes his portrait of people who practice their religion ostentatiously with the sarcastic refrain, *Truly, I say to you, they have received their reward* (vv. 2, 5, 16). The second half of each section, in which Jesus states postively his antidote to the abuse he has described, also ends with a refrain: *and your Father who sees in secret will reward you* (vv. 4, 6, 18).

This section uses the literary resources of satire, as Jesus begins each unit by ridiculing the way in which ostentatious people go about practicing their religion to be seen by people. As is typical of satirists, Jesus exaggerates the practices of those he is attacking, picturing them as having a band of trumpet players precede them when they make their offering (6:2) and as disfiguring their faces to make sure that people know they are fasting (6:16). The positive advice that Jesus offers as a corrective also employs hyperbole, as in the picture of not letting one's right hand know what the left hand is doing when giving alms (6:3), or going into a closet to pray (6:6, KJV).

It is in the middle of this satiric section that Jesus places "the Lord's Prayer" (6:9–13). In its original context, this prayer is offered as a satiric norm—a model of short prayer instead of the *empty phrases* that the Gentiles *heap up* (6:7). The prayer itself adheres to two principles of Jesus' speech: it is in poetic form, and it is aphoristic.

The instruction on practicing religion secretly in the presence of God instead of openly to impress people has as its sequel a threefold exhortation to choose heavenly or spiritual values over earthly values (6:19–24). Jesus does not speak in abstractions but in images of treasure, rust, thieves, light, darkness, servants, and masters. Antithesis underlies the contrasts between earthly and heavenly treasures, light and darkness, and the two masters (God and mammon). Each of the contrasts is climaxed by a memorable proverb that clinches the point: *for where your treasure is, there will your heart be also* (v. 21); *if then the light in you is darkness, how great is the darkness* (v. 23); *you cannot serve God and mammon* (v. 24).

The Discourse Against Anxiety

From two passages dealing with multiple subjects Jesus moves to another extended passage, the famous warning against being anxious (6:25–34). The passage is a lyric meditation in which we contemplate the futility and evil of worry from every possible angle. If we are looking for a masterpiece of persuasive rhetoric, here it is. Jesus pours out reasons and affective appeals to make us *feel* how wrong and useless it is to worry.

Jesus begins by stating his thesis, which he applies to two areas of life (food and clothing):

> Therefore I tell you,
> do not be anxious about your *life*,
>   what you shall *eat*
>   or what you shall *drink*,
> nor about your *body*,
>   what you shall *put on*.

Then Jesus asks a twofold rhetorical question that repeats the two subjects that have been introduced:

> Is not *life* more than *food*,
>   and the *body* more than *clothing*?

Jesus next takes up the first of the two topics that he has introduced, the subject of food. He bases his argument on an analogy from nature and clinches the point by persuasively adding a rhetorical question with which we cannot possibly disagree:

> Look at the birds of the air:
>   they neither sow nor reap nor gather into barns,
>   and yet your heavenly Father *feeds* them.
> Are you not of more value than they?

Still more persuasion follows as Jesus asks another rhetorical question, which this time forces us to acknowledge how ineffectual worry is:

> And which of you by being anxious
>   can add one cubit to his span of life?

Having disposed of the conventional reasons for worrying about food, Jesus proceeds to his second announced topic, clothing. Again he uses an analogy from nature, saying, in effect, "Take a look around you and observe God's providence":

>And why are you anxious about *clothing*?
>Consider the lilies of the field, how they grow;
>>they neither toil nor spin.

Not only are the lilies clothed without effort on their part, but the beauty of their clothing is even greater than that of Solomon, the Old Testament touchstone for magnificence:

>yet I tell you,
>even Solomon in all his glory
>was not *arrayed* like one of these.

Then Jesus proceeds to apply a second analogy, also taken from nature:

>But if God so *clothes* the grass of the field,
>>which today is alive
>>and tomorrow is thrown into the oven,
>will he not much more *clothe* you,
>>O men of little faith?

In a summary statement, Jesus returns to the categories of experience in which, as he has proved, worry is useless:

>Therefore do not be anxious, saying,
>"What shall we *eat*?" or
>"What shall we *drink*?" or
>"What shall we *wear*?"

Two further reasons explain why these questions are so ignominious:

>For the Gentiles seek all these things;
>and your heavenly Father knows that you need them all.

The positive antidote to the anxiety about physical provision that Jesus has attacked is stated as a proverb:

>But seek first his kingdom and his righteousness,
>and all these things shall be yours as well.

Having refuted all possible counterarguments, Jesus states with finality the conclusion toward which his argument has been pointing:

> Therefore do not be anxious about tomorrow,
> for tomorrow will be anxious for itself.

To conclude the entire discourse, Jesus offers an aphorism that implies a note of gentle cynicism and compassionate realism about what life in a fallen world is like:

> Let the day's own trouble
> be sufficient for the day.

In this meditation on the futility of worry we see the *affective* nature of Jesus' discourses. By the time we finish listening to Jesus' case against worry, we are left feeling that it is the last thing in the world that we would care to do.

Three Religious Practices

In the next section we return to the threefold arrangement. Jesus here provides instruction about judging others (7:1–5), witnessing (7:6), and prayer (7:7–12). The aphoristic and poetic tendencies of Jesus' discourses here combine to achieve an effect that is both memorable and eloquent:

> with the judgment you pronounce
>   you will be judged,
> and the measure you give
>   will be the measure you get. [7:2]

> Do not give dogs what is holy;
>   and do not throw your pearls before swine. [7:6]

> Ask, and it will be given you;
> seek, and you will find;
> knock, and it will be opened to you.
>   For every one who asks receives,
>   and he who seeks finds,
>   and to him who knocks it will be opened. [7:7]

Who can doubt that Jesus is one of the world's most famous poets? No poet has been more quoted than Jesus.

Three Great Contrasts

As Jesus concludes his oration (7:13–27), he sharpens the issues and begins to force a response from his listeners. He leaves his audience with a challenge, urging them to make sure that they are members of God's kingdom. In order to make his point with impact, Jesus uses three memorable contrasts—the narrow gate that leads to life versus the wide gate that leads to destruction (vv. 13–14), true prophets versus false prophets (vv. 15–23), and the wise man who builds his house on a rock versus the foolish man who builds on the sand (vv. 24–27).

Jesus' mastery of metaphor and simile is much in evidence here at the end of his most famous public speech. Life is a path with a gate at the entrance. False prophets are ravenous wolves in sheep's clothing. Prophets are like fruit trees that can be judged by their fruit. Hearing or rejecting the words of Jesus is like building a house. Jesus the teller of parables here merges with Jesus the poet.

We do not need the epilogue (7:28–29) to tell us that Jesus was a master orator. It does, however, confirm my earlier claims about the strongly dramatic cast of much of the New Testament. The prologue to the Sermon on the Mount situates the speaker in a definite landscape and before a specific audience: "Seeing the crowds, he went up on the mountain, and when he sat down his disciples came to him" (5:1). As the curtain falls at the end of the sermon, we observe the crowd again: "And when Jesus finished these sayings, the crowds were astonished at his teaching" (7:28).

Jesus' Sermon on the Mount epitomizes his oratorical style. That style is proverbial, poetic, and patterned. Jesus did not scorn literature but flaunted his mastery of it.

Paul's Address in Athens

The second major repository of orations in the New Testament is the Book of Acts. In fact, three-fourths of the book consists of speeches and their immediate settings.[1] Modern scholarship has repeatedly shown that the orations of Acts are cast into the rhetorical forms common in classical culture of the time. F. F. Bruce divides the speeches of Acts into four main categories—evangelistic, deliberative, apologetic, and hortatory.[2]

One of the most memorable speeches in Acts is Paul's address to the Areopagus in Athens (Acts 17:16–33). The Athenian address has evoked disagreement from modern scholars. In particular, scholars have been troubled by the need to reconcile Paul's seeming approval of the pagan assumptions of his audience with the uncompromising

1. I take this figure from Paul Schubert, "The Final Cycle of Speeches in the Book of Acts," *Journal of Biblical Literature* 87 (1968): 16.
2. F. F. Bruce, *The Speeches in the Acts of the Apostles* (London: Tyndale, 1942).

Christian witness that is customary in his preaching. I believe that the key to the interpretation of the Athenian address lies in a literary approach, that is, one which pays close attention to the narrative details given in Acts and which places the oration in the context of the rules of classical rhetoric and oratory.

The Context of the Oration

The narrative tells us what we need to know about the circumstances in which the oration occurred. We learn, for example, that the thing that prompted Paul to speak was his horror at the idolatry that he saw around him: "Now while Paul was waiting . . . at Athens, his spirit was provoked within him as he saw that the city was full of idols" (v. 16). The people who cleared the way for Paul to speak were "the Epicurean and Stoic philosophers" (v. 18). This means that Paul was addressing an intellectual audience, not the people on the street with their crude idolatry.

There has been disagreement about what is meant by the statement that Paul was brought "to the Areopagus" (v. 19) to deliver his address. The Areopagus was both a hill and a council of men who exercised control over the public speaking that went on in Athens. There would seem to be good evidence for concluding that Paul spoke before this council or court, having been asked to demonstrate his credentials as a speaker in the marketplace. We read that Paul stood "in the middle of the Areopagus" (v. 22). At the end "Paul went out from among them" (v. 33), indicating that Paul stood before a group of men known as "the Areopagus."

If we realize that the address was delivered to a dignified council, we are in a better position to understand the drama of the occasion and the reason for the dignity of Paul's address. His oration adheres to the best form of classical oration and includes allusions to Homer, Plato, and other Greek writers.

The narrative framework also informs us that the oration was cut short by the interruption of the audience. It is often claimed that the address as it has been recorded in Acts is a summary of a much longer address. If we look closely at the text, however, this conclusion appears doubtful. The dignified opening of the address shows no sign of being condensed. The style is leisurely and drawn out. The sentences and clauses are long and include parallel constructions (vv. 24–25, 29). The address as we have it even includes Paul's quotations from Greek poets. Furthermore, verse 32 states clearly that "*when* they heard of the resurrection of the dead, some mocked." In other words, at a specific point in the address the audience made it impossible for Paul to continue.

Classical Rhetoric in the Address

The narrative context, when combined with an awareness of the structure of a classical oration, gives us the key to interpreting the Athenian address. According to classical rhetoric, the first part of an address was the *exordium*. This was the introduction to the main part of the speech. According to Quintilian, a contemporary of Paul, the aim of the exordium was "to prepare the hearer to listen to us more readily in the subsequent parts of our pleading. This object, as is agreed among most authors, is principally effected by three means, by securing his good will and attention, and by rendering him desirous of further information."[3] The introduction, in short, was designed to ingratiate the speaker with his audience. A common way of gaining the attention of the listeners was to cite some anecdote that would interest them.

The recorded oration of Paul to the Areopagus is virtually all exordium. In it, Paul pours his energies into establishing rapport with his listeners—saying things with which they agreed, finding a common base with them, making his audience feel that they had begun their quest for God with the right conception. Having done all this, Paul intended to add the Christian distinctives to this introduction. But he never had a chance to develop the main part of his address, as we shall see.

Paul begins his dignified oration with the formula that the famous Athenian orator Demosthenes used to open his addresses: *Men of Athens* (v. 22). Paul's intellectual audience would have felt on native ground with such an opening.

Paul next gives an assessment of the character of the Athenians, appealing to the interest that every audience has in how a visitor views them: *I perceive that in every way you are very religious* (v. 22). This is a commendation and an attempt to find common ground between Paul and his audience. The word translated "religious" could mean either "superstitious," with negative connotations, or "religious," with positive connotations. Obviously Paul is using it in the favorable sense as part of his strategy of gaining a sympathetic hearing.

Paul next uses the time-honored technique of recounting an anecdote, in this case one that involved the listeners themselves: *For as I passed along, and observed the objects of your worship, I found also an altar with this inscription, "To an unknown god"* (v. 23). Then Paul announces his topic: *What therefore you worship as unknown, this I proclaim to you* (v. 23). Paul here defines his audience very carefully. He

---

3. Quoted from Kenneth Myrick, *Sir Philip Sidney as a Literary Craftsman* (Lincoln: University of Nebraska Press, 1965), p. 55.

is addressing philosophers or anyone else for whom the altar to the unknown god summed up their religious state of mind. An altar to an unknown god implies people who have religious sensitivity, who believe that there is a god, but who have not yet found this god. The inscription would appeal to someone dissatisfied with, and skeptical of, the existing religious climate. Paul is appealing to such people, playing on their dissatisfaction and building upon it.

As Paul proceeds to talk about the God who he and his audience agree exists, he first stresses something with which his intelligent audience would agree—that God cannot be confined in physical idols:

> The God who made the world and everything in it, being Lord of heaven and earth, does not live in shrines made by man, nor is he served by human hands, as though he needed anything, since he himself gives to all men life and breath and everything. [vv. 24–25]

We must bear in mind that Paul is addressing persons who are dissatisfied with the existing idol worship, as evidenced by their declaration that their god is still an unknown god.

As Paul continues, he talks about what we might call universal theism. He claims that there is a universal divine being, that people have a religious consciousness, and that people who seek God can find him:

> And he made from one every nation of men to live on all the face of the earth, having determined allotted periods and the boundaries of their habitation, that they should seek God, in the hope that they might feel after him and find him. Yet he is not far from each one of us. [vv. 26–27]

There is nothing distinctively Christian about Paul's remarks thus far. Paul is simply closing ranks with his audience, assuring them that they share with him an awareness that there is a God and that together they can know this God. The word translated "feel after" may have struck a familiar note in Paul's Greek audience. Homer had used the word to describe the groping of the blinded Cyclops Polyphemus as he sought the entrance of his cave, while Plato had used it in the *Phaedo* to describe people's guesses at the truth.[4]

By now Paul's audience is hearing what it likes to hear in the style it likes best. As Paul proceeds, he continues to emphasize that he

---

4. Based on E. M. Blaiklock, *The Acts of the Apostles: An Historical Commentary* (Grand Rapids: Eerdmans, 1959), pp. 144–45. My subsequent references to Paul's allusions come from the same source.

shares the theism of his audience. In fact, he quotes with approval from several Stoic poets who had expressed the same idea:

> "In him we live and move and have our being";
> as even some of your poets have said,
> "For we are indeed his offspring." [v. 28]

One source to whom Paul may be alluding here is Cleanthes, who had written, "Thou, Zeus, art praised above all gods. . . . The origin of the world was from thee: and by law thou rulest over all things. Unto thee may all flesh speak, for we are thy offspring." The Greek poet Aratus had written, "Always we have need of Zeus. For we are also his offspring. . . ." And the poet Epimenides had written about Zeus, "For in thee we live and are moved and have our being." The fact that the brief exordium of Paul's oration contains so many echoes of Greek authors is testimony to Paul's Greek education and to the dignity of the occasion. It also makes very doubtful that we have a shorthand summary of his speech.

As Paul nears the end of his exordium, he summarizes the general points that he has made:

> Being then God's offspring, we ought not to think that the Deity is like gold, or silver, or stone, a representation by the art and imagination of man. [v. 29]

The style of the speech up to this point has been exalted, leisurely, allusive, and repetitive—the opposite of what it would be if the speech as recorded in Acts were a condensation.

Having completed the exordium, Paul moves to the part of his oration that Latin rhetoricians would have called the *propositio*—the statement of thesis. Here at last Paul begins to declare the distinctives of the Christian faith—things such as repentance, judgment, Jesus, and eternal life. As a transition between the exordium and the Christian thesis that he hopes to develop, Paul says, *The times of ignorance God overlooked, but now he commands all men everywhere to repent* (v. 30).

The next verse continues the statement of the thesis that Paul has come to defend:

> because he has fixed a day on which he will judge the world in righteousness by a man whom he has appointed, and of this he has given assurance to all men by raising him from the dead. [v. 31]

Paul has now warmed to his theme and is ready to develop his Christian message. And what happens? He is interrupted and cannot continue: "Now when they heard of the resurrection of the dead, some mocked; but others said, 'We will hear you again about this' " (v. 32). The next verse confirms that Paul's speech was cut short: "So Paul went out from among them" (v. 33), with the word *so* connecting Paul's departure from the group with the mocking of some of his listeners.

The Aftermath of the Speech

The epilogue to the story of Paul's address hints that the interrupted oration was not a total failure: "But some men joined him and believed, among them Dionysius the Areopagite and a woman named Damaris and others with them" (v. 34). One of Paul's converts was "Dionysius the Areopagite," a member of the Areopagus, whose name was also used by famous mystic of the early Christian church.

How did Paul evaluate his oratorical performance before the Areopagus? There is evidence that he may have been disillusioned with his attempt to impress his listeners with his high-flown address that never got beyond the introduction. Paul's next stop on his missionary journey was Corinth (Acts 18:1). In a letter that he later wrote to the Corinthian church, Paul described two kinds of preaching: "When I came to you, brethren, I did not come proclaiming for you the testimony of God in lofty words or wisdom. For I decided to know nothing among you except Jesus Christ and him crucified" (1 Cor. 2:1–2).

Although we cannot be certain about the point, Paul might well be alluding to this address before the Areopagus. He describes how when he came to Corinth he made a conscious decision not to preach in "lofty words or wisdom" (that is, purely human wisdom) and not to preach about anything except the distinctively Christian subject of "Jesus Christ and him crucified."

We must not be misled, however, into thinking that Paul's sermons and writing are not rhetorically accomplished. He may have bid a farewell to the embellishments of classical rhetoric in his preaching, but his defense speeches recorded later in Acts adhere to the conventions of similar orations in the classical world.[5] Furthermore, Paul's style, even in passages where he repudiates human wisdom and eloquence, is a rhetorically sophisticated style, as we shall see in the next section.

5. See Fred Veltman, "The Defense Speeches of Paul in Acts," in *Perspectives on Luke-Acts*, ed. Charles H. Talbert, Special Studies, no. 5 (Danville, Va.: Association of Baptist Professors of Religion, 1978), pp. 253–56.

1 Corinthians 13

The gap between New Testament oratory and the Epistles is very small. The authors of the Epistles were preachers whose sermonic rhetoric carried over into their writing. The audiences of their sermons and letters were essentially the same. The New Testament epistles circulated in oral form among the churches, and many of them were written with such a context in mind.

To illustrate the oratorical style of the New Testament epistles, I have chosen to explicate 1 Corinthians 13. My governing purpose is to show how patterned, how eloquent, and how artistic the passage is. The implied thesis of this entire book is that the New Testament is a literary and artistic book, and that we have heard far too much about its unliterary nature. My analysis of 1 Corinthians 13 should demonstrate that Paul's pejorative comments about human eloquence do not mean that his own writing is anything less than very eloquent.

The genre of 1 Corinthians 13 is the encomium, a lyric passage that praises an abstract quality. The subject of this encomium is love. The passage praises its subject by means of the usual formulas of an encomium: the indispensability of the subject (vv. 1–3), a catalogue of its praiseworthy acts and attributes (vv. 4–7), the superiority of love (vv. 8–13), and a concluding command to emulate the subject (14:1— "Make love your aim").

The poem of praise comes to us in an oratorical, wavelike style in which the organizing principle is repeated patterns of three. Balance, parallelism, and contrast are also much in evidence.

The passage opens with three parallel statements, each of which falls into a threefold formula. The formula is this: (1) *If I . . .*, (2) *but have not love*, (3) *nothing* (or an equivalent). Each of the units is thus based on an all-or-nothing contrast:

> If I speak in the tongues of men and of angels,
>   but have not love,
>   I am a noisy gong or clanging cymbal.
> And if I have prophetic powers,
> and understand all mysteries and all knowledge,
> and if I have all faith,
> so as to remove mountains,
>   but have not love,
>   I am nothing.
> If I give away all I have,
> and if I deliver my body to be burned,
>   but have not love,
>   I gain nothing.

This is both highly artistic and oratorical. It is the kind of passage that asks to be read aloud.

The next movement, the catalogue of love's acts and attributes, is also based on a rhetorical pattern of three. In three successive clauses, the noun *love* is the subject of verbs that follow it:[6]

> Love is longsuffering,
> is kind;
> love envieth not;
> love vaunteth not itself,
> is not puffed up,
> doth not behave itself unseemly,
> seeketh not its own,
> is not easily provoked,
> imputeth not the evil;
> rejoiceth not at unrighteousness,
> but rejoiceth with the truth;
> beareth all things,
> hopeth all things,
> endureth all things.

An oratorical passage like this enters our consciousness in a series of waves. It is rhythmic and affective, sweeping us along with its eloquence.

The pattern of threes continues in the next unit, which contrasts the permanence of love with the transience of three spiritual gifts (which, incidentally, have already been introduced in the opening movement of the passage):

> Love never ends;
> as for prophecies, they will pass away;
> as for tongues, they will cease;
> as for knowledge, it will pass away.

The same contrast is elaborated in the next unit, where the word *imperfect* occurs three times as well:

> For our knowledge is imperfect
> and our prophecy is imperfect;
> But when the perfect comes,
> the imperfect will pass away.

6. English translations tend to obscure the rhetorical pattern in this section. My version is based on Henry Alford, *The New Testament for English Readers* (Chicago: Moody, n.d.).

For further elaboration of the motif that the imperfect is inferior to that which is perfect and therefore permanent, Paul introduces the analogy of what he was like as a child as contrasted with what he is like as an adult:

> When I was a child,
>   I spoke like a child,
>   I thought like a child,
>   I reasoned like a child.
> When I became a man,
>   I gave up childish ways.

Balance and contrast continue as Paul applies the analogy to the announced topic of spiritual gifts that will pass away, as opposed to love, which endures:

> For now we see in a mirror dimly,
>   but then face to face.
> Now I know in part,
>   then I shall understand fully,
>   even as I have been fully understood.

The threefold pattern accompanied by contrast reaches its climax in the famous aphorism with which the discourse concludes:

> So faith, hope, love abide, these three;
>   but the greatest of these is love.

What this shows, I trust, is that the oratorical style of the New Testament epistles deserves some of the epithets that we commonly ascribe to literature: beautiful, eloquent, and artistic. Augustine was right when he said that "wisdom was [Paul's] guide, eloquence his attendant."

8

The Book of Revelation

The Book of Revelation is the most thoroughly literary book in the Bible. It is filled with images, characters, and events.[1] Ironically, it is also the book of the Bible that commentators have tried the hardest to translate out of its literary mode into an expository or propositional mode.

The Literary Genres of the Book of Revelation

The Book of Revelation is an anthology or compendium of literary genres. The combination of literary forms that converge in the book makes it unique, but this should not be allowed to obscure the fact that the forms themselves are familiar ones. If we simply take the time to piece together the separate strands in the book, there is no reason why we should find it a perplexing book.

The two broadest categories of literature are story and poetry. In any strict sense, the Book of Revelation is neither, but an easy familiarity with narrative and poetry are the best preparation for under-

1. Some excellent commentary on the literary nature of the Book of Revelation can be found in various sources collected in Leland Ryken, ed., *The New Testament in Literary Criticism*, A Library of Literary Criticism (New York: Ungar, 1984), pp. 302–28.

standing the book. Also prominent are the genres of drama, epistle, apocalypse, and epic.

The Book of Revelation as Story

Overall, the Book of Revelation is conceived on a narrative principle. This is partly obscured by the fact that the story is told as a series of visions instead of in a smooth narrative flow. But the visions fit together the way episodes in a story do.

As in any story, there is a unifying plot conflict in the Book of Revelation. The overarching conflict is a spiritual struggle between good and evil. Within this general framework, we find a whole system of contrasts at work. There are many character conflicts, for example: Christ versus Satan, the saints versus the followers of the beast, the bride of Christ versus the whore of Babylon, the Lamb versus the dragon, Michael's angels versus the dragon's angels. Scenic contrasts are equally pervasive: heaven versus the sinful earth and the bottomless pit, the city of God versus "the great city" of evil, New Jerusalem versus Babylon.

There are also conflicting actions. The establishment of the New Jerusalem is set against the destruction of Babylon. The sealing of the saints has as its counterpart the receiving of the mark of the beast. Most of the individual visions, moreover, are structured as a conflict between forces of good and evil. Nor should we overlook a basic temporal contrast that underlies the book, a contrast between timeless eternity (associated with deliverance for believers) and temporal history (associated with various types of misery).

The linear sequence of the book corresponds to what happens in a story. There are few works of literature that have such a strong onward pressure as the Book of Revelation. We are continually being propelled to the next event as we read. The linear movement is not a smooth narrative flow from one event to the next. The movement is much closer to some of the effects in modern cinema—a kaleidoscopic sequence of visions, pictures, sounds, images, and events, ever shifting and never in focus for very long. The lack of a smooth narrative sweep, combined with the repetitive structure of the book, makes it impossible to arrange the book according to a rigid chronology in which each event is regarded as following the preceding event or scene.

Despite this lack of a single chronology, the Book of Revelation has the sense of progression that we associate with stories. As we progress through the book, we are caught up in a movement through increasingly intense conflicts between good and evil. With the fourth of the seven seals, for example, a fourth of the earth is judged (6:8); with five of the judgments introduced by the seven trumpets, a third (8:7–12);

and with the plagues resulting from pouring of the seven bowls of wrath, the entire earth, "for with them the wrath of God is ended" (15:1). As we near the end of the book, we have the strong sense that the great conflict between good and evil is moving toward its final resolution.

Even more important than the overall plot structure of the book is the way in which the organizing framework for the individual units is a narrative framework. The most helpful way to make sense of the individual units is to ask the following questions, which are the standard narrative questions:

1. The question of setting: *where* does the action occur?
2. The issue of character: *who* are the actors or agents?
3. The question of plot or action: *what* happens?
4. The issue of plot outcome: what is the *result* of the action?

This basic narrative framework will enable us to organize virtually any individual passage in the Book of Revelation.

The Book of Revelation as Drama

Reinforcing the narrative thread of Revelation are its strong affinities with drama.[2] The format of the book—a number of visions—makes it a series of dramatized scenes. Again and again we find characters placed into elaborately described settings. Speeches, songs, and snatches of dialogue punctuate the action. The book is not, of course, a single sustained drama. It is more like a pageant, with brief scenes following each other to produce an overall story of the end of history.

We might remember in this regard that the New Testament world was essentially a Greek world. Greek civilization had for centuries been known for its drama. People were familiar with the conventions of the theater. Although never intended for the stage, the Book of Revelation is cast into a form that would be familiar to anyone who thought in terms of the theater. The book should also seem accessible to a century (our own) in which people automatically have the right antennae to assimilate works that resemble television dramas and films.

The Epistolary Framework

Although story and drama provide the dominant organizing framework for the book, these are not the first things to greet us as we start

2. See John W. Bowman, "The Revelation to John: Its Dramatic Structure and Message," *Interpretation* 9 (1955): 436–53.

to read. John chose as his portal into the book a familiar New Testament form—the epistle or letter. "John to the seven churches that are
in Asia," we read in the fourth verse of the book. This is the customary
salutation of the New Testament epistles. Following the prologue,
moreover, we find a total of seven letters to the churches (chaps. 2–3).
John has obviously adapted a popular form of early Christian literature.

The epistolary framework reappears at the very end of the book
(22:6–21). The miscellaneous admonitions and concluding thoughts
resemble those at the end of most New Testament epistles. Balancing
the opening salutation of the book is the concluding benediction: "The
grace of the Lord Jesus be with all the saints. Amen" (22:21). Someone
has rightly said that "Revelation is, in fact, the first book to show the
influence of the collected and published letters of Paul."[3]

The Book of Revelation as Apocalypse

The literary family into which the Book of Revelation is most cus-
tomarily placed is the form known as apocalypse. This form, too, was
familiar to a Hebrew audience of the early Christian era, although it
often seems strange to modern readers. Apocalyptic works are visionary works that transport us to an alternate world from the one in
which we live. Literally the word *apocalypse* means "unveiling," or a
revelation of something that is hidden.

Apocalyptic writing has a number of identifiable characteristics,
virtually all of them fully evident in the Book of Revelation. Apocalyptic works are dualistic in the sense that they divide the world de-
cisively into good and evil. Apocalyptic writing is also eschatological,
being primarily concerned with future events, especially those at the
end of history. The basic unit of presentation is the ecstatic vision of
a world remote from our own, either in time or in the sense of being
a supernatural world.

Biblical apocalypse tends to be messianic, centering in the appearance and work of a divine Messiah. Angels and demons are prominent.
Also common are animal symbolism (use of animals to stand for
human characters, movements, or events) and numerology (use of
numbers with symbolic meanings). Apocalyptic writing tends to be
judgmental, with the writer denouncing an existing system of values
and predicting its miserable end. There can be no doubt that the apocalyptic genre is the dominant form of the Book of Revelation.

Apocalyptic writing is not as remote from our own literary experience as it may seem at first. It has many of the traits of folk literature.

3. Edgar J. Goodspeed, *How to Read the Bible* (Philadelphia: Universal Book and
Bible House, 1946), p. 201.

The presence of animal characters, for example, is something with which we have resonated from childhood. In the Book of Revelation we encounter such animal characters as the Lamb, horses of various colors, warriorlike locusts, a dragon, and terrifying beasts from the sea and earth.

Color symbolism is something else that the popular imagination has always relished. In the Book of Revelation, the color white is associated with Christ (1:14), the saints of God (3:18; 4:4; 7:9, 14; 19:8), the armies of heaven (19:14), and God's throne of judgment (20:11). Red, by contrast, usually appears in contexts of evil—warfare (6:4), the appearance of the satanic dragon (12:3), and the whore of Babylon and her beast (17:3–4).

Even the element of deliberate strangeness in apocalyptic writing has parallels in modern writing. Someone has compared such writing to underground writing in which oppressed people develop a code language of obscure and indirect symbols, which in the case of Revelation "were necessary for the safety of both writer and readers at a time when the church was driven underground by the Roman Gestapo."[4] Someone else believes that the closest parallel in our day is the political cartoon, in which nations or their leaders are represented as animals (the eagle for the United States or the dragon for China) or an stereotyped figures (such as Uncle Sam).[5] It seems reasonable to believe that the "caricatures" in the Book of Revelation would have been immediately recognized by John's original audience. The whore of Babylon, for example, obviously stood for the Roman empire.

The Book of Revelation as Epic

The Book of Revelation is also similar to the narrative genre known as epic. As such, it reminds us of such familiar epics as Homer's *Odyssey*, Virgil's *Aeneid*, and Milton's *Paradise Lost*. Its style, for example, is an epic style. The writer uses epic similes in an effort to do justice to his vision and theme: "his feet were like burnished bronze, refined as in a furnace" (1:15); "a great star fell from heaven, blazing like a torch" (8:10); "a loud voice, like a lion roaring" (10:3).

Another feature of epic style is the exalted epithets (titles) that convey a sense of exuberance: "Jesus Christ the faithful witness, the firstborn of the dead, and the ruler of kings on earth" (1:5); "the Lord God Almighty, who was and is and is to come" (4:8); "King of kings and Lord of lords" (19:16). There are also epic catalogues—of churches, of

4. Charles F. Wishart, "Patmos in the Pulpit," *Interpretation* 1 (1947): 459.

5. G. R. Beasley-Murray, *The Book of Revelation* (London: Marshall, Morgan and Scott, 1974), pp. 16–17.

the beings around God's throne in heaven, of the tribes of Israel, of the jewels in the heavenly city. Epic style achieves grandeur and depth through the presence of allusions, and Revelation is no exception. It contains some 350 allusions to the Old Testament, as well as many references to the redemptive life of Christ.

Epic style is exuberant and overflowing, and here, too, Revelation meets the standard:

> Grace to you and peace from him who is and who was and who is to come, and from the seven spirits who are before his throne, and from Jesus Christ the faithful witness, the first-born of the dead, and the ruler of kings on earth. [1:4–5]

C. S. Lewis has written that "continuity is an essential of the epic style," and he speaks of "the enormous onward pressure of the great stream on which you are embarked." Such a style, adds Lewis, can be described with such terms as "ritualistic," "incantatory," possessing "grandeur," capable of creating "the true epic exhilaration."[6] Such designations describe exactly what we encounter as we read the Book of Revelation.

The content of Revelation is as thoroughly epic as is the style. Epics are stories of great and heightened conflict. They portray battles in which at least some of the participants are spiritual beings using supernatural means of warfare. The setting for the action is cosmic and includes heaven as well as earth and hell. The whole tendency is expansive. The following excerpt from Revelation is thoroughly recognizable as an epic event:

> Then I saw another amighty angel coming down from heaven, wrapped in a cloud. . . . And he set his right foot on the sea, and his left foot on the land, and called out with a loud voice, like a lion roaring; when he called out, the seven thunders sounded. [10:1–3]

Epic abounds in bigger-than-life characters and events.

Other epic conventions are also present in Revelation. There are scenes set in heaven where decisions are made that are then enacted on earth. In function and construction, these scenes are like the epic councils of the gods. Epics usually include a preview of future history, and this is the premise underlying most of the Book of Revelation. Epics recount the exploits of a hero who conquers his enemies and establishes an empire. The Book of Revelation is the epic story of

6. C. S. Lewis, *A Preface to Paradise Lost* (New York: Oxford University Press, 1942), pp. 40, 45–46.

Christ's conquest of Satan and evil and his establishing of his eternal spiritual kingdom.

Symbolism in the Book of Revelation

Cutting across all the genres of the Book of Revelation is the basic literary mode of symbolism. This means that concrete images and events are constantly used to represent something else. Instead of Christ's being pictured as a spirit or man, for example, he is portrayed as a lion and lamb. To interpret such symbols literally is to misread the book.

To insist that the mode is symbolic is not to deny that the Book of Revelation describes historical events that really happen. The question is not whether the events are historical but whether they are described *literally*. The events described by John are historical events that really happen (or will yet happen), but *how* will they happen? Fortunately we have a passage within the book that does not portray future events but is instead a flashback that portrays past events. By observing how the writer handles these recognizable events, we can determine the basic pattern of interpretation that we are intended to apply elsewhere in the book.

This passage occurs in chapter 12 and describes the incarnation of Christ. Here is an excerpt:

> [1]And a great portent appeared in heaven, a woman clothed with the sun, with the moon under her feet, and on her head a crown of twelve stars; [2]she was with child and she cried out in her pangs of birth, in anguish for delivery. [3]And another portent appeared in heaven; behold, a great red dragon, with seven heads and ten horns, and seven diadems upon his heads. [4]His tail swept down a third of the stars of heaven, and cast them to the earth. And the dragon stood before the woman who was about to bear a child, that he might devour her child when she brought it forth; [5]she brought forth a male child, one who is to rule all the nations with a rod of iron, but her child was caught up to God and to his throne.

The writer himself twice calls this brief drama a portent or sign, not a literal account. On the basis of the Old Testament symbols for the tribes of Israel (vv. 1–2), we can identify the woman as Israel. The child who is to rule all the nations is obviously Christ. The dragon, we know, is Satan (12:9), who was unable to destroy Christ during his earthly life and redemptive ministry.

Here, then, we can see the symbolic mode of Revelation: it does not literally describe the circumstances of Christ's birth, *but it calls those circumstances to mind.* This is the interpretive key to the whole book.

We can find this same exegetical key in the visions of the four horses (6:1–8). These four visions together form a unit and are based on the procession motif. Four horses with riders move across our field of vision, and we get a progressively more sinister pageant of warfare. The first horse, a white horse whose rider "went out conquering and to conquer," symbolizes the spirit of warfare, initially somewhat attractive. The next horse is "bright red," the color of blood, and its rider "was permitted to take peace from the earth." This is more sinister than the white horse with a conquering warrior.

The third horse is black, the color of death, and its rider "had a balance in his hand." This is an unusual weapon for a warrior to be carrying, but it is explained by a voice that says, "A quart of wheat for a denarius, and three quarts of barley for a denarius." These prices for the weights of grain make the scene a picture of famine (see Ezekiel 4:9–10 and Leviticus 26:26 for parallels). This surrealistic picture of the destructiveness of war reaches its climax with the fourth horse, yellowish-green in color, "and its rider's name was Death, and Hades followed him."

What does this nightmare vision of warfare really mean? It is a symbolic account of what Jesus predicted directly and propositionally in his Olivet Discourse: "You will hear of wars and rumors of wars. . . . For nation will rise against nation, and kingdom against kingdom, and there will be famines and earthquakes in various places" (Matt. 24:6–7). The four visions have been symbolic of events or movements that really happen, but that do not happen literally as the Book of Revelation pictures them. What Jesus predicted will not literally take the form of four warriors riding on horses, but the symbolic picture of the four horsemen calls those realities to mind.

This symbolism is already present in the seven letters to the churches, which are the most historically rooted part of the Book of Revelation. We read there about the sword of Jesus' mouth (2:16), people not having soiled their garments (3:4), glorified believers becoming a pillar in a temple (3:12), some Christians having become lukewarm (3:16), and Christ standing at a door and knocking (3:20). No one takes these statements literally. They are symbolic of *spiritual* realities. If there is this much symbolism already in the seven letters to the churches, how much more can we not expect in the more visionary chapters that follow?

This symbolic mode is customary throughout the prophetic writings of the Bible. The youthful Joseph dreamed that the sun, moon, and stars bowed down to him. This prophecy was, indeed, fulfilled, but not in the form in which it occurred in the dream. The second chapter of Daniel contains an account Nebuchadnezzar's dream of a human figure composed of various minerals. This symbolic figure stood for political realities, but these realities did not literally consist of various minerals. Isaiah 13:10–13 predicts the fall of Babylon in symbolic terms of the sun and moon being darkened, the heavens trembling, and earth being shaken. The surrounding context makes it clear that the destruction really consisted of military defeat, which verses 10–13 describe symbolically.

This customary biblical mode of symbolism makes a reappearance in the apocalyptic Book of Revelation. A lot of interpretive nonsense will be avoided if we follow the interpretive method that the Bible itself suggests for this type of prophetic writing.

Interpreting the Symbols

If there are this many symbols in the book, how do we know what they mean? This is the central problem in the interpretation of the Book of Revelation. Our best equipment is a keen eye for the obvious. We need to make use of what we know on the basis of our experiences in life and our acquaintance with literature in general. It is important to remember that literary symbolism is a largely conventional and universal language. The purpose of the symbols of Revelation is to reveal, not to conceal. Since the allusions and techniques used in the Book of Revelation are so thoroughly rooted in the Bible as a whole, we should also use what we know about biblical symbolism in general.

Earlier I said that the Book of Revelation gives us symbolic pictures of historical characters, events, and movements. Although the book does not give us a literal account of these things, it does *call them to mind.* A good stock question to ask of any passage in Revelation is therefore this one: *Of what theological fact or event in salvation history does this passage seem to be a symbolic version?*

As an example, consider this passage:

> Then I saw another angel ascend from the rising of the sun, with the seal of the living God, and he called with a loud voice to the four angels who had been given power to harm earth and sea, saying, "Do not harm the earth or the sea or the trees, till we have sealed the servants of our God upon their foreheads." [7:2–3]

What does this picture of the sealing of the believers mean? In biblical symbolism, a seal was a mark of ownership. The sealing of the servants of God on their foreheads is a symbolic picture of believers being claimed and saved by God. Here is the theological fact or event from salvation history that the passage calls to mind.

Or consider this brief picture:

> The fourth angel poured his bowl on the sun, and it was allowed to scorch men with fire; men were scorched by the fierce heat, and they cursed the name of God who had power over these plagues, and they did not repent and give him glory. [16:8–9]

The first thing that we should do with this surrealistic picture of torture is to experience the physical sensations of the event portrayed. The Book of Revelation is a book of images. We need to read it with what modern psychology calls the right side of our brain (our ability to think by means of images and intuition). Having done so, we can ask what recognizable fact of history is pictured here. It is obviously a picture of God's judgment against human sinfulness and of the unrepentant heart as it exists throughout human history. It is as simple (and as profound) as that.

We do not need esoteric road maps to take our journey through the Book of Revelation. We need a firm grip on human experience in the world, on the obvious meanings of literary symbols, and on the theological framework of the Bible as a whole. Whenever something more specific is intended, the book itself will provide the interpretation (for examples, see 1:20; 4:5; 17:7–18; 19:8).

What kind of historical events does the Book of Revelation describe by means of its symbols? There have been four major approaches to the book. One regards the book as arising out of the situation of the first-century church and interprets the events as having occurred in the early centuries of history after Christ. A second interpretation considers the book as forecasting the whole of human history from the time of Christ to his return. A third approach, the futurist, believes that except for the first few chapters the book is exclusively concerned with happenings at the end of history. Finally, the idealist view minimizes the historical particulars of the book and holds that it depicts principles and theological ideas on which God operates throughout history.

I think that the book is a combination of all of these. We should begin with the situation of the church to which the book was written. Because of the literary form of the book, which portrays events symbolically, its relevance extends throughout the history of the world. Babylon, for example, may have been the Roman empire for John's first-century audience, but in Old Testament times it was literally Babylon, and it has taken many forms throughout history. The literary mode of symbolism means that the events portrayed in Revelation are perpetually relevant and will be ultimately relevant at the end of history.

The Nonpictorial Mode of the Book

To insist on the symbolic mode of the book is not to say that it is a strongly pictorial book. The book is strongly sensory and even visual (in the sense that we visualize images and symbols), but not predominantly pictorial. The harder we try to visualize the scenes, the more incomprehensible and grotesque they become. One scholar has put it this way:

> Symbolic writing ... does not paint pictures. It is not pictographic but ideographic. ... The skull and crossbones on the bottle of medicine is a symbol of poison, but not a picture. ... The fish, the lamb, and the lion are all symbols of Christ, but never to be taken as pictures of him. In other words, the symbol is a code word and does not paint a picture.[7]

Thus the description of a sun-clothed, star-crowned woman in chapter 12 is a symbol of the church, not a picture of it.

The description of Christ in the opening chapter is a good test case in this regard:

> [12]Then I turned to see the voice that was speaking to me, and on turning I saw seven golden lampstands, [13]and in the midst of the lampstands one like a son of man, clothed with a long robe and with a golden girdle round his breast; [14]his head and his hair were white as white wool, white as snow; his eyes were like a flame of fire, [15]his feet were like burnished bronze, refined as in a furnace, and his voice was like the sound of many waters; [16]in his right hand he held seven stars, from his mouth issued a sharp two-edged sword, and his face was like the sun shining in full strength.

We do not experience this description as a single composite figure. We assimilate it piecemeal, interpreting each detail in a symbolic way.

The *golden lampstands* amid which Christ stands symbolize the churches to whom the seven letters are about to be addressed. The *long robe* that Christ wears indicates a person of priestly and kingly distinction. The *white hair* suggests ancientness, with the detail modeled on Daniel's picture of the "Ancient of Days" (Dan. 7:9).

7. Donald W. Richardson, *The Revelation of Jesus Christ: An Interpretation* (Richmond: John Knox, 1939), p. 16. For more comments along this line, see the excerpts in *The New Testament in Literary Criticism*, pp. 315–20.

The images of eyes *like a flame of fire* and *feet like burnished bronze* indicate the supernatural or transcendent nature of Christ. They are the first occurrence in the book of enamelled imagery—imagery (especially of jewels and glass) that makes us think of hardness of texture and brilliance of light. Such imagery suggests a spiritual realm whose permanence transcends our cyclic vegetative world. The picture of Christ holding *seven stars* in *his right hand* reinforces this atmosphere of mystery and more-than-earthly magnitude. The *two-edged sword* that protrudes from Christ's mouth symbolizes his judgment against evil. The face *like the sun shining in full strength* likewise resists our picturing it visually and instead *suggests* the power and supernatural splendor of Christ.

This portrait of Christ is primarily a symbolic rendition in which individual details stand for some quality of Christ. It is intended to be not representational but impressionistic. It conveys a sense of Christ's awesomeness, eternity, splendor, power, judgment, and mystery, but cannot be said to be a picture of those things. The theological significance of this technique is important. A literary critic analyzed the difference between the statues of Greek gods and the impressionistic description of God in Revelation and came to this conclusion:

> When one thinks of the serenity of the Greek representations of the gods beside these visions of the Hebrew and Christian seers, the latter at first may seem confused and turgid. Then as one thinks it over the very clarity and definiteness of outline in these wonderful marbles stand out as a limitation: in comparison with these vague and mystical imaginings of the Christian seers the representations of Greek art are impotent. In the end the Greek statue of a god, for all its gracious beauty, is only a glorified and idealized man. The visions of the apocalypse, on the other hand, transcend once for all the limitations of human nature.[8]

Archetypes

Many of the images and symbols in the Book of Revelation belong to the familiar archetypes of literature. The world of the book is an elemental world of life, death, blood, lamb, dragon, beast, light, darkness, water, sea, sun, war, harvest, white, scarlet, bride, throne, jewels, and gold. There are many references to rising, usually associated with spiritual goodness, and falling, associated with evil. Heaven is high and light, while the bottomless pit is low and dark.

The last half of the book is a spiritualized version of familiar archetypes: a woman in distress who is marvelously delivered, a hero

8. J. H. Gardiner, *The Bible as English Literature*, in *The New Testament in Literary Criticism*, p. 320.

on a white horse who kills a dragon, a wicked prostitute who is finally exposed, the marriage of the triumphant hero to his bride, the celebration of the wedding with a feast, and the description of a palace glittering with jewels in which the hero and his bride live happily ever after. Underlying the entire book is a submerged journey motif, as human history painfully winds its way toward its goal and consummation.

Structure and Unity in the Book of Revelation

Despite its multiplicity of individual visions, the Book of Revelation is the most carefully structured long work in the Bible. I have already suggested some pathways through the book: a unifying plot conflict between good and evil, a progressive movement toward the final resolution, and a repeated pattern consisting of scene/agent—action—result.

Although the work is constructed on a repetitive principle in which we retrace a similar cycle of events, the background story that these cycles reenact has a definite organization to it. It is the same pattern of events that Jesus outlines in the Olivet Discourse (Matt. 24–25). We can organize the pattern into five phases:

1. Wars, earthquakes, famine, and false teachers (Matt. 24:5–8).
2. Persecution of Christians (Matt. 24:9–22).
3. False Christs and false prophets (Matt. 24:23–28).
4. Natural disasters, the appearance of Christ, and the harvesting of the elect (Matt. 24:29–31).
5. Final judgment (Matt. 24:32–25:46).

The Book of Revelation tells the same story as this, and does so a number of times. It fills in the details beyond what Jesus does in the Olivet Discourse, but we can make sense of what is happening in any given unit of Revelation simply by relating the foreground events to this general pattern in the background.

There are so many details in Revelation that we might well despair of being able to keep it in our mind as a single entity. But upon analysis the book turns out to have a simple and manageable structure. The outline of the book consists of a prologue, a series of six sevenfold units, and an epilogue. Here is the outline of the book:

1. Prologue (chap. 1).
2. Letters to the seven churches, climaxed by a vision of heaven (2–4).

3. The seven seals:
   a. prologue (5).
   b. warrior on a white horse (6:1–2).
   c. warrior on a red horse (6:3–4).
   d. rider on a black horse (6:5–6).
   e. Death riding on a pale horse (6:7–8).
   f. martyrs in heaven (6:9–11).
   g. cosmic dissolution, associated with God's judgment (6:12–17).
   h. interlude: sealing of the 144,000, a picture of the glorified saints (7:1–17).
   i. silence (8:1).
4. The seven trumpets:
   a. prologue (8:2–6).
   b. hail, fire, blood on the earth (8:7).
   c. the sea becomes blood, and destruction at sea (8:8–9).
   d. the falling star, bringing bitter water (8:10–11).
   e. darkening of sun, moon, and stars (8:12).
   f. locusts from the pit (8:13–9:12).
   g. the cavalry of judgment (9:13–20).
   h. interlude: John eats the scroll; the history of the two witnesses, persecuted and triumphant (10:1–11:14).
   i. judgment and glorification of believers in heaven (11:15–19).
5. The seven great signs:
   a. the dragon's war against the Son, the woman, and the woman's offspring (12).
   b. the beast from the sea (13:1–10).
   c. the beast from the earth (13:11–18).
   d. the Lamb on Mount Zion (14:1–5).
   e. angelic messages of judgment (14:6–13).
   f. the reaping of the earth (14:14–16).
   g. reaping and judgment of the wicked (14:17–20).
6. The seven bowls of wrath:
   a. prologue (15).
   b. sores on men (16:1–2).
   c. sea becomes blood (16:3).
   d. rivers become blood (16:4–7).
   e. fierce heat of the sun (16:8–9).
   f. darkness (16:10–11).
   g. the foul spirits prepare for Armageddon (16:12–16).
   h. earthquake and final judgment against evil (16:17–21).
7. The seven events of final judgment and consummation:
   a. judgment of Babylon (17–18).
   b. marriage supper of the Lamb (19:1–10).

    c. Christ defeats the beast and the false prophet (19:11–21).

    d. the binding of Satan and the millennial reign of Christ (20:1–6).

    e. the loosing of Satan and his defeat (20:7–10).

    f. final judgment (20:11–15).

    g. description of the new heaven and new earth (21:1–22:5).

  8. Epilogue (22:6–21).

This scheme is like a road map through the book. No matter where we are, we can locate ourselves somewhere in a landscape of sevenfold events.

But the unity is even tighter than this. Each of the sevenfold units is composed of two basic ingredients—fallen human history, closely associated with evil and judgment, and the consummation of history, often linked particularly with the glorification of believers in heaven. Furthermore, the general movement within each unit is from fallen human history with its evil and misery to consummation (in the form of either the end of history or the glorification of believers in heaven). From earth to heaven, from history to its end—this is the recurrent movement in the units that make up the Book of Revelation. No matter where we dip into the book, we know where we are.

The Book of Revelation is one of the easiest books to read in the Bible. It is an affective book. It feeds our imaginations with heightened images of judgment, splendor, redemption, mystery, good and evil, battle, heaven, and worship.

Reading the Book of Revelation

Although the Book of Revelation has a strongly repetitive or cyclic structure in which we repeatedly encounter the same sequence of events, it is also a progressive book. In fact, we are unlikely to read another book where so much happens so quickly. The purpose of the running commentary that follows is to capture something of the flow of the action, as well as to provide some preliminary interpretation of the events and symbols.

The Epic Prologue

The opening chapter of the book is an epic prologue or introduction. Any grand event begins with ritual and formality. The Book of Revelation begins in exactly this way and in a manner that resembles the openings of epics. The opening chapter is a fourfold introduction to the book. First we are introduced to the theme and source (vv. 1–3). Then the writer greets his audience with a formal salutation (vv. 4–8). Finally we are introduced to the narrator of the book (vv. 9–11) and to the hero (vv. 12–20).

Epic writers begin by announcing their theme or subject. "Of man's first disobedience," writes Milton at the beginning of *Paradise Lost*. John begins his book with a similar announcement: *The revelation of Jesus Christ* (1:1). In the story that follows, Christ will stand revealed in all his glory. This is the content of John's book. Epic poets also begin by invoking a deity or muse to inspire them. John does not invoke God but does the equivalent by identifying God as the divine source for his work: *The revelation of Jesus Christ, which God gave him to show to his servants . . . by sending his angel to his servant John, who bore witness to the word of God* (1:1–2). The next verse pronounces a blessing (one of seven beatitudes scattered throughout the book) on the person *who reads aloud the words of the prophecy, and . . . those who hear*. Oral performance is yet another epic feature of Revelation.

With the formal salutation (vv. 4–8) the epic style and content of the book come into fuller view. I have already noted the exuberance and grandeur of the style of the passage. At the level of content, epic motifs such as *kingdom, glory,* and *dominion* are now fully established as the expectations that we bring to the ensuing action.

In the final two units of chapter 1, the narrator and hero step forward. The narrator is like that in other epics—a mediator between his audience and a vision of supernatural characters and events, a representative of his audience ("John, your brother, who share with you in Jesus the tribulation and the kingdom and the patient endurance"), an agent of divine inspiration. And in keeping with the opening promise that the book will reveal Jesus Christ, in the symbolic portrait of Jesus that concludes the chapter the hero stands revealed in all his power and splendor.

The Letters to the Churches

As his gateway into the main part of his revelation, John chose the familiar New Testament form of the epistle. Chapters 2 and 3 are letters to seven representative churches. The artistry of the letters is amazing. In keeping with the pattern of seven that typifies the book as a whole, the individual letters fall into a sevenfold pattern, as follows:

1. *A greeting* ("To the angel of the church in . . .").
2. *A title for Christ* (with all but the last one taking some detail from the description of Christ in chapter 1).
3. *A commendation of the church* (beginning, "I know . . .").
4. *A criticism of the church* (omitted in the cases of Smyrna and Philadelphia).
5. *A warning.*

6. *An exhortation to be attentive* (beginning with the statement "he who has an ear, let him hear . . .")
7. *A promise* (beginning with a formula to the effect "to him that overcometh will I give . . ." [KJV]).

In the last four letters, the order of items 6 and 7 is reversed, introducing an element of variety into the overall pattern.

Although the letters are addressed to particular churches, their content is timeless and universal. Together the letters embody the themes that are important to the Book of Revelation as a whole. The letters show that there is a great spiritual conflict going on in the world. Everyone is involved. The forms of evil differ from one church to another, but they are essentially variations on the theme of good versus evil, Christ versus Satan. In one way or another, some kind of positive choice for Christ is demanded in every letter. People's response to the call to godly living is a matter of momentous importance, with a person's eternal welfare at stake.

Another theme in the letters is that God is the sovereign judge who is concerned about what people are doing in the world. People are urged to live in an awareness of God's presence, and the certainty of God's judgment is repeatedly offered as the rationale for repentance while there is time. There is, finally, a repeated emphasis on the fact that Christ is coming again. In the letters, Christians are enjoined to live in an eschatological awareness, ordering their lives around the certainty of Christ's return. Because life has a goal, patient endurance becomes a chief mark of the Christian in these letters.

In terms of the narrative framework that we can apply to any section of Revelation, the main scene of action is earth, more specifically seven representative cities (an archetype that will be important throughout Revelation, incidentally). The agents are the followers of Christ and the followers of Satan. The action consists of the church encountering conflict, persecution, and false doctrine. The result, as implied in the concluding promise "to him that overcometh," is that people choose their eternal destiny.

Taken together, the letters speak of the same events that Jesus outlines in his Olivet Discourse. There are references to persecution of believers, false teachers within the churches, the return of Christ, and final judgment. The individual letters also reveal the general movement that I have claimed for all the sevenfold sections of Revelation—a movement from history, associated with trial and misery, to the spiritual realities that will be ushered in at the end of history.

Chapter 4, a scene of heavenly worship, is often considered to be an independent interlude or a prelude to the opening of the seals in the next chapter. It can more plausibly be interpreted as the climax of the movement that underlies the letters to the seven churches. These letters have ended with brief but undeveloped pictures of heavenly reward for the faithful. In chapter 4, these foreshortened visions of heaven finally receive their consummation. The opening verse of chapter 4 confirms this: the vision that follows is a picture of *what must take place after this,* that is, after the events described in the letters.

Chapter 4 itself is one of the great visions of Revelation, suffused with supernatural splendor. The imagery and symbolism convey a general aura of glory but also invite more specific interpretation. There is combined specificity and vagueness in the opening vision of *a throne . . . in heaven, with one seated on the throne* (v. 2). Enamelled images dominate our impression:

> And he who sat there appeared like jasper and carnelian, and round the throne was a rainbow that looked like an emerald. [v. 3]

Modeled on a similar vision in Ezekiel (1:27–28), the light and rainbow convey the impression of an encircling brightness around the throne. Again we move between clarity and vagueness, specific description and reticence.

With God established as the still center around which heavenly ritual occurs, the description moves to the surrounding action. First a heavenly court is assembled in our imaginations as we read:

> Round the throne were twenty-four thrones, and seated on the thrones were twenty-four elders, clad in white garments, with golden crowns upon their heads. [v. 4]

Then we see *flashes of lightning* and hear *peals of thunder* (v. 5), archetypes for the presence and power of God. To climax the effect, we see in our imaginations *a sea of glass, like crystal* before the throne (v. 6).

And this is only the beginning. As our gaze moves still further outward from the throne, we see *four living creatures, full of eyes in front and behind* (v. 6). At such a point we become acutely aware that the descriptive mode is symbolic, not pictorial. These are obviously symbols of watchfulness and omniscience. The four creatures are then specifically identified with the lion, ox, man, and eagle (v. 7). The important thing about these creatures is probably their superlative power and excellence, as in a rabbinic saying that "the mightiest among the birds is the eagle, the mightiest among the domestic animals is the bull [ox], the mightiest among the wild beasts is the lion, the mightiest among all is man." We have here the best in God's creation, offering praise to God.

With the dramatic stage props now assembled, heavenly praise is introduced into the scene (vv. 8b–11). Brief lyric fragments like this will recur throughout the Book of Revelation and add a note of emotional response appropriate to the content of the book. Indeed, heavenly experience would be incomplete without this note of singing that makes the Book of Revelation, in its own way, the New Testament book of psalms.

The Seven Seals

The next sevenfold unit in Revelation is the series of seven seals that are opened as predictions of future events. The unit begins with a prelude set in heaven (chap. 5). Chapter 5 is a self-contained unit with a single setting (the heavenly court), a central action (the declaration of the worthiness of the Lamb to open the scroll), and a unifying theme (the worthiness of Christ). Applying the narrative framework of scene/agent—action—result, we can say that the scene is heaven, the chief agent is Christ, the action is that by a process of elimination only Christ is able to open the seals of the scroll, and the result is that with the obstacle overcome we are propelled into the actual series of visions. In function and construction, the scene resembles the heavenly council in epics, where action is initiated in heaven and then enacted on earth.

Symbolism pervades the scene, and there is no attempt at a single consistent picture. In one verse (5) Christ is pictured as a lion and in the very next verse (6) he is a lamb. These are symbols of Christ, not pictures of him. The lion symbolizes power and kingship, while *the Lamb standing, as though it had been slain* (v. 6) symbolizes the atonement of Christ. This scene of heavenly ritual rises to a crescendo of praise, beginning with the four creatures and twenty-four elders around the throne (v. 8), then encompassing all the heavenly hosts of angels and saints (v. 11), and finally extending to *every creature in heaven and on earth and under the earth and in the sea* (v. 13). The passage has a strong linear movement and is conceived dramatically (with elaborate attention to both scene and dialogue). Like the other visions of Revelation, this one mingles the familiar and the unfamiliar to produce its supernatural effect.

We next move to the opening of the seven seals. The first four visions (6:1–8) form a unit. As suggested in my earlier discussion of this passage, the four vignettes of horse and rider are a pageant or procession in which the spirit of warfare, initially attractive, becomes a nightmare of misery and destructiveness on earth. These visions present in visual and symbolic form the warfare and famine that Jesus predicted in his Olivet Discourse.

From this vision of catastrophe on earth, the focus suddenly shifts to heaven, where the martyrs are pictured awaiting God's vengeance against the forces of evil (6:9–11). The martyrs, whom I take to be symbolic of believers in general, are placed in a symbolic setting (under a heavenly altar). The souls of these believers ask for justice on earth, but the justice that they request is postponed. The souls are consoled by being given *a white robe,* symbolic of their victory in heaven. The overarching conflict between good and evil in the book as a whole here takes the form of a prediction that justice will not occur *until the number of their fellow servants and their brethren should be complete, who were to be killed as they themselves had been.*

The sixth seal (6:12–17) brings the shift from fallen history, with its miserable warfare and famine, to the consummation of history. We get a vision of cosmic collapse replete with powerful archetypes of the end—a great earthquake, a black sun and bloody moon, stars falling to the earth, the sky vanishing like a scroll, and every mountain and island being removed from its place. The inhabitants of the earth respond by fleeing from the wrath of the Lamb. It is not hard to identify the reality that is pictured by means of these images and symbols. This is the end of history and the final judgment that we read about throughout the Bible.

The subsequent interlude in which believers are *sealed* (chap. 7) completes the movement from earthly history to heavenly bliss. The sealing of the believers is a symbolic action that identifies these persons as belonging to God. It is the great opposite of the receiving of the mark of the beast by unbelievers (13:16). The sealing is dramatized as occurring on a heavenly stage. It unfolds in two stages: first John hears the number of the sealed (v. 4) and then he sees the multitude of the redeemed (v. 9). The number of those sealed (144,000) is symbolic of completeness and hugeness. All twelve tribes are present, with the foursquare symbolism of twelve times twelve reinforcing the sense of completeness that we feel with the number 144,000. The number of a thousand was the ancient equivalent for the largest number imaginable.

The scene of heavenly celebration that concludes chapter 7 typifies the scenes of celebration and worship that are interspersed throughout the book. We are greeted with a flood of idealized archetypes, which are uniquely powerful in the Book of Revelation. There are white robes of triumph and joy, a throne of God to suggest his kingly rulership in heaven, a temple to symbolize God's presence, springs of living water to express the satisfaction of every human need, and much in addition.

The seventh seal (8:1) surprises us: instead of a further vision, there is simply *silence in heaven for about half an hour.* The Book of Revelation is full of surprises and mysteries like this. Throughout the book clarity and mystery mingle. We are given enough to satisfy us, but enough is also withheld to leave us with a longing to know more.

Looking back over the vision of the seven seals, we can see how manageable the units in Revelation are. A great deal happens, leading me to note that in the Book of Revelation the sheer amount of what happens is out of proportion to the brevity of the text. The account of the seven seals began with the vision of four horses, then the martyrs were comforted in heaven and told of more persecution on earth, then the earth dissolved before the judgment of Christ, and finally the complete host of the redeemed was glorified in heaven.

One pattern underlying the section is the movement from history, associated with misery, to the consummation of history, associated with judgment against unbelievers and the glorification of believers in heaven. A second pattern is the outline of events that Jesus gives in the Olivet Discourse: first wars, famine, and persecution; then natural disasters and the appearance of Christ; then final judgment and glorification. A third organizing framework is the narrative framework that pervades the book: the scene is earth and heaven, the agents are God and all people, the action is the destruction of earth and the glorification of believers in heaven, and the result is the end of evil and the perfection of good.

The Seven Trumpets

The vision of the seven trumpets (chaps. 8–11) follows the same general pattern as that of the seven seals, emphasizing the cyclic structure of the book as a whole. Again there is a preliminary scene set in heaven, where God's judgment against the evil earth is decreed (8:3–6). The four visions of horses here have their parallel in four visions involving the elemental aspects of nature—earth, sea, rivers, sun, moon, and stars (8:7–12). These elemental forces are used to convey the impression that something basic is happening in the earthly sphere. The sense of calamity is more terrifying than with the fourth seal, for the fourth part of the earth affected there (6:8) is now replaced by a third part of the earth, sea, rivers, and sun, moon, and stars.

The fifth trumpet (9:1–11), involving the opening of the bottomless pit, is the most terrifying image of evil yet to appear in the unfolding drama of Revelation. This pit, with its archetypal associations of descent (it is bottomless), smoke, and darkness (9:2), is an image from our nightmares and evokes primitive feelings of horror and revulsion. Pictured as an abyss with a narrow opening at the top, the pit is a hell-like place, if not a picture of hell itself.

The locusts that ascend from the pit are agents of God's judgment against unbelievers (9:4). They are a biblical archetype, recalling similar judgments of God in the eighth plague against the Egyptians and against the Israelites in the prophecy of Joel. In one of the most amazing imaginative feats of a book filled with them, the terror of the locusts is amplified when the writer links a literal locust with other threatening forces (9:7–11). The locusts are *like horses arrayed for battle*, not in terms of size, but because they come in droves and with destructive effect, just as war-horses do. Their teeth are *like lions' teeth*, not literally, but in their destructive potential as they devour standing grainfields. The hard shell of a locust's body becomes amplified into *iron breastplates*, and the literal noise with which plagues of locusts sweep the countryside becomes amplified by the writer's imagination into *the noise of many chariots with horses rushing into battle*.

The sixth trumpet, which pictures a cavalry of warriors (9:13–21), is one of the most mysterious episodes in the book. The purpose of the cavalry is clear: the troops are agents of God's judgment to *kill a third of mankind* (v. 15). They are thus part of the overriding conflict between good and evil. But much is left unexplained. The cavalry is introduced into the narrative abruptly (v. 16), as though we already know who they are, but in fact we do not know whether they are human or angelic warriors. The war-horses, like the locusts of the previous vision, become transformed into bigger-than-life apocalyptic creatures. Their mouths eject fire, smoke, and sulfur (vv. 17–18), and their tails are like serpents with heads (v. 19). Balancing this physical terror is the moral and spiritual terror of unrepentant humanity with which the vision concludes (vv. 20–21).

The interludes introduced into the visions of the seals and trumpets are major passages, in effect small, self-contained apocalypses. The interlude of the two witnesses between the sixth and seventh trumpets (10:1–12:13) is an example. Its narrative effect, like that of the interlude between the sixth and seventh seals, is to generate suspense, as the climactic seventh vision is momentarily withheld. Perhaps we are to see in this that repentance is possible while God withholds his final judgment.

The interlude in the section about the trumpets begins with one of the "giantesque" scenes of Revelation: a mighty angel descends from heaven and stands with his right foot on the sea and his left foot on the land. His voice is like that of a lion roaring. The mystery of all this is reinforced when John is told to eat the scroll that the angel carries. The mystery hardly dissipates when we know that there are parallel moments with the Old Testament prophets Jeremiah (15:16) and Ezekiel (3:1–3). Many of the events and images of Revelation apparently exist to reveal the sheer mystery of the spiritual world. The simultaneous bitterness and sweetness of the scroll when John eats it (10:9–10) underscore the dual nature of John's prophecy, which is comforting to believers but bitter in its pronouncement of judgment upon evil.

The story of the two witnesses (11:1–13), also part of the interlude, is itself a reenactment of the history of believers that occurs elsewhere in Revelation. These two figures, symbolizing the believing church, are given the task of proclaiming God's word in a degenerate time of history. They are associated with olive trees (see Zechariah 4:14 for the source of the symbol), symbolizing life in the midst of death, and lampstands, symbolizing light in the midst of darkness. The two figures are also linked by way of allusion with Moses and Elijah, as evidenced by their ability to prevent rainfall, to turn water into blood, and to bring about plagues (11:6). The symbolism of all this is clear: the church in persecution has the same resources available to it as the Old Testament prophets had.

From the opening description of the two prophets we move to their epic feat. It consists of proclaiming God's word (v. 7). Following an epiclike battle in which the beast kills the two witnesses (v. 7), there is a scene of exultant evil followed by the miraculous revival of the witnesses. This sequence of events either pictures a single event that will occur near the end of history, or it is a vision of the archetypal pattern of what happens whenever the defeated church revives. In either case, the story of the two witnesses has reenacted the basic motif of Revelation—persecution of the church in a corrupt world followed by eventual triumph. In the words of Austin Farrer, the interlude of chapter 11 "is a foreshortened and premature conclusion, cancelled, and yet permitted to stand by way of interlude."[9]

The seventh trumpet (11:15–19) brings this section of the book to an expected climax, modeled along the lines of earlier climaxes. History is consummated when *the kingdom of the world has become the kingdom of our Lord and of his Christ* (v. 15). The coming of Christ to establish his kingdom is accompanied by the judgment of all the dead, good and evil (v. 18), in the manner predicted by Jesus in his Olivet Discourse and his eschatological parables. A riot of sensations forms the conclusion of the episode:

> Then God's temple in heaven was opened, and the ark of his covenant was seen within his temple; and there were flashes of lightning, loud noises, peals of thunder, an earthquake, and heavy hail. [v. 19]

The Book of Revelation never fails to fill our imaginations. In the terms

9. Austin Farrer, *A Rebirth of Images: The Making of St. John's Apocalypse* (London: Dacre, 1949), p. 44.

popularized by contemporary psychology, here is a book that speaks to the right side of the brain (the hemisphere that assimilates images).

The Seven Great Signs

Chapter 12, which initiates the section of the seven great signs, in several ways summarizes the whole Book of Revelation. It opens with a symbolic account of the birth of Christ (vv. 1–5) and a description of how a great red dragon (symbolizing Satan) attempts to destroy him. The child's miraculous ascension into heaven (v. 5) is a symbolic way of depicting Satan's inability to destroy Christ during his earthly life. As I suggested earlier, this section is a flashback, not a forecast. Because it deals with recognizable historical events, it serves as the interpretive key for Revelation, showing us that the writer uses symbols that bring literal events to mind.

As the defeat of Satan continues to unfold in this first great sign, the scene shifts from earth to heaven. The picture of a war in heaven, with *Michael and his angels fighting against the dragon* (v. 7), epitomizes both the epic quality of the Book of Revelation and the overriding plot conflict of the Bible as a whole. Satan's being cast out of heaven (v. 9) might well be a symbolic account of Christ's victory at Calvary, along the lines of Christ's prediction before his crucifixion that "now shall the ruler of this world be cast out" (John 12:31). Having been cast out of heaven, the dragon concludes the episode by going off *to make war* on the offspring of the woman (that is, the church), and *on those who keep the commandments of God and bear testimony to Jesus* (v. 17). Here is the flashback that explains what happens elsewhere in the Book of Revelation.

This vision involving the woman and dragon alerts us to the essentially imaginative mode of Revelation. It is a book that requires a childlike response. A woman clothed with the sun, with the moon under her feet and a crown on her head, a great red dragon who is cast out of heaven, a dragon pouring water out of its mouth and thereby threatening a woman who is miraculously rescued when the earth opens its mouth and swallows the stream—these are events that speak to what is childlike in our imaginations. We have encountered this type of thing in our reading of fantasy literature.

Chapter 13 is divided between two further signs, those involving a beast from the sea (vv. 1–10) and a beast from the earth (vv. 11–18). The symbolism associated with the beasts shows that they are counterfeits of Christ. One of the heads of the beast from the sea, for example, *seemed to have a mortal wound, but its mortal wound was healed, and the whole earth followed the beast with wonder* (v. 3). This is the demonic counterfeit of the dying and reviving Christ. Similarly, the beast from the earth *had two horns like a lamb* (v. 11), giving it a resemblance to the Lamb of God depicted elsewhere in Revelation. In addition, the mark that is put on the right hand or the forehead of the beast's followers (v. 16) echoes the earlier sealing of the believers as a mark of their possession by God.

I said in my introductory remarks that the symbolic mode of the book requires us to ask, Of what theological reality or event in salvation history does this detail seem to be a symbolic version? The two beasts of chapter 13, with their ability to counterfeit, to persecute, and to lead people astray, should remind us of a prediction that Jesus made in the Olivet Discourse: "For false Christs and false prophets will arise and show great signs and wonders, so as to lead astray, if possible, even the elect" (Matt. 24:24).

As we have come to expect, the sequence of seven great signs in the middle of Revelation moves from what will happen on earth to a vision of ultimate victory for believers in heaven. Chapter 14 accordingly opens with a vision of the Lamb on Mount Zion, symbolic of Christ in heaven. The redeemed, the great opposite of the followers who bear the mark of the beast, are described by means of two evocative symbols. They are compared to chaste men *who have not defiled themselves with women* (14:4). This male image complements the more familiar image of the church as a chaste bride. As with the image of the bride later in Revelation, we find here a metaphor in which sexual purity symbolizes that believers are pure in their devotion to Christ. The believers in heaven are also described as those who have been *redeemed from mankind as first fruits for God and the Lamb* (14:4). In Hebrew sacrifices, the first fruits were the choicest part of a harvest, set aside as a special offering to God. The body of the redeemed is said to be set aside to God in a similar manner.

The remainder of chapter 14 is devoted to scenes connected with the end of history. They include messages predicting God's coming judgment of evil (vv. 6–13), Christ's reaping of the earth (vv. 14–16), and the final judgment of the wicked (vv. 17–20). These visions come alive in our imaginations by means of some of the great archetypes of evil and judgment—Babylon the great, the wine of God's wrath, the smoke of torment, the reaping of the earth with a sickle, and the winepress of God's wrath, with blood flowing from it so deep that it reaches a horse's bridle. Here is the essential mode of Revelation—a phantasmagoria of images, some of them possessing all the terror of a surrealistic nightmare.

Chapters 12–14, beginning with the incarnation of Christ and concluding with his second coming, "provide a complete apocalypse."[10] Like the seven letters, seals, and trumpets, these chapters display a

10. Ibid., p. 53.

movement from the flow of history to events that will culminate history and bring triumph to believers. It is evidence of the cyclic structure of the book as a whole, and of its tendency to repeat common themes and patterns in new ways. As I said at the outset, once we grasp the essential movement of the individual units of the book, we are never at a loss. We can step into any section of the book and know our way around.

The Seven Bowls of Wrath

The section about the seven bowls of wrath (chaps. 15–16) repeats the usual pattern. The judgments are described briefly so as not to belabor the issue. This vision is prefaced with a heavenly council (chap. 15), just as the visions of the seals and trumpets were. As in the earlier sequences, moreover, the plagues center on elemental nature and human warfare. Along with this repetitive element, there is progression, as we are informed of the finality of judgment this time: these plagues *are the last, for with them the wrath of God is ended* (15:1).

This vision is devoted wholly to the theme of God's judgment, both during history and at its consummation. The pouring out of the first five bowls (16:1–11) pictures God's judgment on elemental nature, with most of the details resembling those of the ten plagues against Egypt in the Book of Exodus. Pouring of the sixth bowl (16:12–16) describes, without giving the details, a climactic battle between good and evil that will occur at Armageddon. Here is another of the epic events in the Book of Revelation. From history we move to its consummation, as pouring the seventh bowl (16:17–21) echoes such eschatological images from elsewhere in the Bible as earthquake, lightning, thunder, cities splitting apart, and islands and mountains vanishing.

The Seven Last Events

Chapters 17–22 bring to a conclusion all of the smaller, tentative cycles that have preceded. Because of the progressive intensification that has accompanied the unfolding action in Revelation, we read this last sevenfold cycle with a strong impression that this is the final version of judgment against evil and the triumph of good.

This great drama of judgment begins with the single most extended vision in Revelation—the judgment of the whore of Babylon (chaps. 17–18). The drama unfolds in three stages, as we move from an opening description of the harlot (17:1–6a) through an explanation of her significance (the remainder of chap. 17) to a prediction of her punishment (chap. 18). The whore of Babylon is another of the great symbols of Revelation. On the literal level, she is described as *seated upon many waters* (17:1). She is also pictured as a city. Since in the Old Testament Jeremiah had addressed the city of Babylon as "you who dwell by many waters" (Jer. 51:13), it is evident that John is modeling his symbolic Babylon along the lines of the Babylon of ancient times.

In Revelation, however, it is the symbolism that counts. Babylon emerges in our imaginations as both a corrupt city and a monstrous woman. The color symbolism of red (17:3–4) already sets up negative connotations, which become reinforced when the woman is described as a prostitute *with whom the kings of the earth have committed fornication* (v. 2). And these are only the beginning. As the recital of immoralities continues, the kings are also described as having become drunk with the wine of fornication (v. 2). Cannibalism is the climactic detail: *And I saw the woman, drunk with the blood of the saints and the blood of the martyrs of Jesus* (v. 6). Even the harlot's name elicits horror: *Babylon the great, mother of harlots and of earth's abominations* (v. 5).

Now that we have encountered the whore of Babylon as concrete image and symbol, we are ready for a more analytic account of her. In the remainder of chapter 17, John interprets her significance in both spiritual and political terms. Spiritually she is linked with Satan, as evidenced by the way in which she rides on a beast identified as Satan (v. 7). Politically she is associated with the Roman empire, as suggested by the detail that *the seven heads are seven mountains on which the woman is seated* (v. 9). This was undoubtedly the chief contemporary significance of the symbol for the original audience of the book. By making the heads and horns symbolic of political rulers (vv. 10–12), the angelic interpreter gives this image of evil an ever-expanding set of meanings. And when we finally learn that the various kings *will make war on the Lamb* (17:14), it becomes clear that the image is intended to be a universal embodiment of the principle of evil.

What, then, is represented by the woman, who is also said to be *the great city* (17:18)? She is the human race in community in rebellion against God. In the Old Testament era one form of such evil was Babylon. In John's day, it was Rome. It has taken many forms since then, and it will assume an ultimate form at the end of history.

The entire eighteenth chapter announces the coming doom of Babylon. It belongs to a familiar type of satire found in Old Testament prophecy, the doom song. The lament of the world over Babylon (18:9–19) describes her as a worldwide commercial empire. The references to contemporary Rome are unmistakable in the description, but the picture is also as up to date as our own daily newspaper. While the evil world laments the collapse of its system, heaven rejoices over the fall of Babylon (18:20), reminding us of the great conflict that will rage to the very end of Revelation.

The effect of the two chapters devoted to Babylon is suffocating. With relief we turn to the second of the last signs, the marriage supper of the Lamb (19:1–10). The virginal bride of Christ, dressed in *fine linen, bright and pure* (v. 8), is the great opposite of the whore of Babylon clad in red. In place of the lament of the nations in the preceding vision, the singing of four songs of praise punctuates the brief account of the marriage supper. The triumphal archetype that dominates the conclusion of Revelation—the marriage of a conquering hero to a bride—is now firmly established in our imaginations.

The next three visions are built around the motif of warfare and conquest. They are a vision of Christ as a conquering warrior, defeating the beast and false prophet (19:11–21), the binding of Satan for a thousand years, accompanied by the millennial reign of Christ (20:1–6), and a final battle between the forces of good and evil, ending with defeat of Satan (20:7–10). These are epic events, large and mysterious and awe-inspiring, mingling clarity and mystery.

With the defeat of evil complete, the sequence moves to the final judgment (20:11–15). The picture is filled out with familiar biblical archetypes of judgment—God seated on a great white throne, the disappearance of the earth and sky, multitudes of the dead resurrected and standing before the throne, the opening of the books of deeds and the book of life, and the lake of fire.

The final climax, culminating many earlier and foreshortened climaxes in Revelation, is the description of the new heaven and new earth (chaps. 21 and 22). These pages are uniquely powerful and moving. There is nothing like the effect anywhere else. These paragraphs are a veritable repository of ideal archetypes, including the water of life, the dazzling brightness of light, the secure city, and paradisal plants along a flowing river. There is a wealth of enamelled images to suggest the preciousness and permanence of the place: jasper, crystal, sapphire, and many others. Complementing these positive archetypes are the moving negations of fallen experience: no more tears, death, pain, darkness, or falsehood.

Quite apart from the specific details, the sheer abundance takes on a symbolic value. The detailed account of the heavenly city is an implied rejoinder to the descriptions of Babylon that darkened two earlier chapters. The foursquare measurements of the city (21:16) symbolize its completeness, as does the emphasis on twelve—twelve gates, twelve angels, twelve tribes, twelve foundations, twelve apostles (21:12–14). Overriding all else is the symbolic richness—of dimension, of design, of decoration, of detail.

The Grand Finale to the Bible

The last two chapters of Revelation are the grand climax not only of the Book of Revelation but of the Bible as a whole. At the end of a work of literature we look for a sense of the resolution of the issues that have been introduced. This feeling of closure is exactly what we get at the end of Revelation, and it consists of two motifs—the sense of an ending and the sense of a beginning. After all those biblical stories and poems and visions that portray the havoc that evil brought into human experience, we are assured that the forces of evil have been destroyed. But there is also a sense of new beginnings. The language is reminiscent of Genesis 1 and 2, the archetype of new beginnings. Here at the end of the Bible we are surrounded by the atmosphere of a new heaven and a new earth.

A second ingredient of literary conclusions is a reminder or echo of the beginning—something that leads us to recall where the story began. At the end of a story, it is natural to remember where it all started. This strategy is especially crucial in the Bible, which begins with a perfect world and where any true resolution of the conflict between good and evil must be in some sense a return to the beginning. The first two chapters of the Bible and the last two are like frames around the history of fallen history. Satan enters the story in the third chapter and exits in the third chapter from the end. We begin with a recreation of the world that was created in early Genesis. The paradisal imagery of the opening verses of Revelation 22 takes us back to the first paradise: "then he showed me the river of the water of life . . .; also, on either side of the river, the tree of life with its twelve kinds of fruit, yielding its fruit each month."

Finally, great and momentous stories leave things where they did not begin. At the end, we are aware of the progress that has occurred. In this connection we should contrast the garden that stands at the beginning of the Bible and the city with numberless hosts that stands at the end. There is a sense of completeness with the city whose gates are always open that is not present in the picture of the first two humans living in an enclosed garden. The one is a beginning, the other an ending. The garden is a memory, the city a hope.

Here at the end of the Bible we can see its overall structure, which stretches from creation to apocalypse. The Bible truly begins at the beginning and concludes with the end. It is a complete whole, the story of all things.

Epilogue

Several conclusions emerge from this literary introduction to the New Testament. One is that the New Testament is a thoroughly literary book. It is a book of the imagination in which religious truth is more often embodied in such literary forms as story, metaphor, and symbol than it is expressed in theological abstraction. The New Testament is not a collection of essays, nor a theological outline with proof texts attached, but an anthology of literary genres—narrative, epistle, vision, poem, proverb, parable, and oration.

The literary form that dominates the New Testament is narrative or story. Five of the longest books (the four Gospels and the Book of Acts) are essentially narrative. The Book of Revelation uses a series of visions to tell a story. The Epistles contain snatches of narrative as well.

But the narrative quality of the New Testament extends beyond specific books to the theological content of the New Testament as a whole. New Testament theology is conceived as a story possessing the usual narrative ingredients. The religious reality about which New Testament authors speak and write is a story of what God has done in Christ. This story tells about a great spiritual battle between good and evil, Christ and Satan. This conflict makes choice an inevitable part of the lives of the characters in the story. This story of the soul's choice is full of danger, accompanied by the momentous possibility of either triumph or tragedy.

The central event in the story is a great rescue that Christ accomplished when he defeated Satan by his atoning death and resurrection. The story is built around some great archetypes, including death-rebirth, testing, pilgrimage, and the happy ending. Even the most overtly theological parts of the New Testament keep telling us about this story—about the plot conflict, about the characters involved, about the final goal toward which the action is headed.

The chief means by which this story is told is drama. There is very little summarized narrative in the New Testament. Except for the Epistles, we find such staples of drama as directly quoted dialogue, characters speaking in specific settings to specific listeners who respond, and addresses such as sermons, orations, and defenses.

This dramatic flavor is closely linked with oral forms. The book that we read sprang from a culture that relied on oral transmission of its tradition and stories. This partly explains the characteristic brevity of literary forms that make up the New Testament: the anecdote, the parable, the letter occasioned by a specific problem, the speech, the vision, the hymn. The New Testament books are mainly *collections* of separate units, a fact that makes the books seem longer than they really are and that explains why we find it hard to experience them as unified wholes.

The oral nature of the New Testament extends beyond its genres to its style. That style is frequently dramatic and oratorical. It relies heavily on pattern and repetition. It is aphoristic or proverbial, with the result that much of it stays in the memory. The New Testament is a book that to this day reads aloud amazingly well.

The analysis that I have provided in this literary introduction to the New Testament confirms that the New Testament is an artistic book. Its literary beauty is indisputable. The artistry and compositional skill of its authors must have been partly conscious. Although the New Testament bears all the signs of popular or folk literature, as I conducted many of my explications I saw no way to avoid the conclusion that the New Testament also shows many signs of literary sophistication and polish. Its affinities with the larger world of literature, ancient and modern, are often striking.

The New Testament emerges finally as a paradoxical book. It is a book filled simultaneously with theology and with everyday human experience. It is an intellectual book that requires our best powers of thought, and at the same time an affective book that moves us deeply. Its writers frequently disavow worldly sophistication, yet they produce literature of unsurpassed beauty and stylistic splendor. The New

Testament is a book that communicates a surface meaning to any honest inquirer but also continues to perplex scholars who devote a lifetime of study to it. As the epigraph of this book indicates, the New Testament is a book that can "speak to the people all the words of this Life" (Acts 5:20)—the life that we live in the world and the spiritual life in Christ that the New Testament exists to proclaim.

Glossary

Allegory. A work of literature in which some or all of the details have a corresponding other meaning and refer to either a concept or historical particular.

Allusion. A reference to past history or literature.

Antagonist. The force(s) or character(s) with which the protagonist of a story is in conflict.

Antithetic parallelism. A two-line poetic unit in which the second line states the truth of the first in the opposite way or introduces a contrast.

Aphorism. A short, memorable statement of truth (p. 103).

Apocalyptic literature. A type of Hebrew visionary literature (pp. 138–39).

Apostrophe. A figure of speech in which the writer addresses someone absent or something nonhuman as if it were present or human and could respond to the address.

Archetype. An image, plot motif, or character type that recurs throughout literature and is part of a reader's total literary experience.

Calling stories. In the Gospels, stories in which Jesus calls a person to follow him or to respond to a command (pp. 36–37). Also called *vocation stories.*

Comedy. A story with a U-shaped plot in which the action begins in prosperity, descends into potentially tragic events, and rises to a happy ending.

Conflict stories. Gospel stories that narrate Jesus' controversies with an opposing person or group (pp. 38–39). Also called *controversy stories.*

Didactic. Having the intention or impulse to teach.

Discourse. An address to an audience.

Encomium. A work of literature that praises an abstract quality or a generalized character type.

Encounter stories. Gospel stories in which a person is confronted with the claims of Jesus, which that person must either accept or reject (p. 38).

Epic. A long narrative having a number of conventional characteristics (pp. 139–41).

Epiphany. A moment of heightened insight.

Epistle. A letter that attains literary status by virtue of the literary techniques used in it (pp. 93–97).

Epithet. An exalted title for a person or thing.

Explication. The literary term for close reading of a text. It implies not only careful analysis of a text but also putting one's analysis into organized form for written or oral presentation to an audience.

Foil. Something within a work of literature that heightens or sets off a main element in the work. A foil is usually a contrast (either a character, event, or image), but sometimes it is a parallel.

Folk literature. Literature couched in the language of everyday speech and appealing to the common person (pp. 62–63). Also called *popular literature.*

Genre. A literary type or kind.

Hero. A protagonist who is exemplary and representative of a whole community.

Hybrid forms. Gospel stories that combine elements of one or more genres.

Hyperbole. A figure of speech in which a writer uses conscious exaggeration for the sake of effect, usually emotional effect.

Image. Any concrete picture of reality or human experience, including any sensory experience, a setting, a character, or an event.

Imagination. The human capacity for image-making and image-perceiving.

Irony. An incongruity or discrepancy. There are three main types of literary irony. Dramatic irony occurs when a reader knows more about what is happening than characters in a story do. Verbal irony occurs when a writer states something but means exactly the opposite. Irony of situation occurs when a situation is the opposite of what is expected or appropriate.

Lyric poetry. Short poems containing the thoughts or feelings of a speaker. The emotional quality, even more than the reflective, is usually considered the differentia of lyric.

Metaphor. A figure of speech in which the writer makes an implied comparison between two phenomena.

Miracle stories. Gospel narratives that focus on miracles that Jesus performed (pp. 39–40).

Motif. A discernible pattern composed of individual units, either in a single work or in literature generally.

Narrative. A story; a series of events.

Narrator. The character or "voice" of the writer as it exists in a work of literature.

Occasional literature. A work of literature that takes its origin from a particular historical event or a particular situation in the writer's life.

Parable. A brief narrative that explicitly embodies one or more themes (pp. 62–67).

Paradox. An apparent contradiction that upon reflection is seen to express a genuine truth; the contradiction must be resolved or explained before we see its truth.

Parallelism. Two or more lines that form a pattern based on repetition or balance of thought or grammar.

Parody. A work of literature that parallels but inverts the usual meaning of a literary genre or a specific earlier work of literature.

Passion stories. Gospel stories that narrate the events surrounding the trial, death, and resurrection of Jesus (p. 40).

Personification. A figure of speech in which human attributes are given to something nonhuman, such as animals, objects, or abstract qualities.

Plot. The sequence of events in a story, usually based on a central conflict and having a beginning, middle, and end.

Poetic license. Figurative language that is not literally true or factual.

Pronouncement stories. A brief Gospel story in which an event in Jesus' life is linked with one of his memorable sayings (p. 39).

Protagonist. The leading character in a story, whether sympathetic or unsympathetic.

Proverb. A concise, memorable expression of truth (pp. 106–7).

Quest stories. Stories built around progress toward a goal.

Rhetorical question. A figure of speech in which the writer asks a question whose answer is so obvious that it is left unstated; a question asked, not to elicit information, but for the sake of effect, usually an emotional effect.

Satire. The exposure, through ridicule or rebuke, of human vice or folly.

Saying. A proverb or aphorism.

Simile. A figure of speech in which the writer compares two phenomena, using the explicit formula *like* or *as.*

Stairstep parallelism. A type of parallelism in which the last key word of a line becomes the first main word in the next line.

Symbol. Any detail in a work of literature that in addition to its literal meaning stands for something else.

Synonymous parallelism. A type of parallelism in which two or more lines state the same idea in different words but in similar grammatical form; the second line repeats the content of all or part of the first line.

Synthetic parallelism. A type of parallelism in which the second line completes the thought of the first line, but without repeating anything from the first line. Also called *growing parallelism.*

Theme. A generalization about life that a work of literature as a whole implies or embodies.

Tragedy. A narrative form built around a calamity stemming from a protagonist's wrong choice.

Type scene. A situation or set of conventions that recurs throughout a work of literature or body of literature and that therefore produces a set of expectations in the readers when they encounter that situation in a literary text.

Wisdom literature. A branch of biblical literature in which the writer depends heavily on the proverb as the basic unit.

Witness stories. Gospel stories in which either Jesus or another character testifies about Jesus or his works (pp. 37–38). Also called *testimony stories.*

Index of Subjects

Index of Authors

Index of Scripture